Teacher Talk!

The Art of Effective Communication

Cheli Cerra, M.Ed. & Ruth Ja

JOSSEY-BASS
A Wiley Imprint
www.josseybass.com

D1418346

Published by Jossey-Bass
A Wiley Imprint
989 Market Street, San Francisco, CA 94103-1741 www.josseybass.com

Jossey-Bass books and products are available through most bookstores. To contact Jossey-Bass directly call our Customer Care Department within the U.S. at 800-956-7739, outside the U.S. at 317-572-3986 or fax 317-572-4002.

Jossey-Bass also publishes its books in a variety of electronic formats. Some content that appears in print may not be available in electronic books.

ISBN: 0-471-72014-3

Printed in the United States of America

10 9 8 7 6 5 4 3 2 1

The Buzz About Teacher Talk!

"Teacher Talk! provides fast savvy advice to help teachers master all of the challenges of working with parents. The worksheets alone are worth any teacher's time and money."

Dr. Michael White, *Director of Educational Consulting Services and licensed Pediatric Psychologist, National Consultant for the Center for Performance Assessment.*

"This book is an absolute winner. Teachers and prospective teachers will benefit greatly from the proven, practical information and easy-to-implement suggestions. Apply the information and see your teaching career soar!"

Annette Breaux, Author of *101 Answers for New Teachers and Their Mentors,* co-author with Elizabeth Breaux of *Real Teachers, Real Challenges, Real Solutions,* and co-author with Dr. Harry K. Wong of *New Teacher Induction: How to Train, Support, and Retain New Teachers.*

"A great workbook that makes sense for college students on the educational track. This book is as good as it gets."

Dr. Richard Cohen, *Dean, Ross College of Education, Lynn University.*

More Buzz About
Teacher Talk!

"Teachers will love these easy-to-apply tips and real-life strategies they can use immediately with students, administrators, teachers, and parents. The authors provide helpful worksheets, assessments, and sample dialogue so you have everything you need to communicate effectively."

Sam Horn, *Author of* Tongue Fu® *and* Take the Bully by the Horns.

To Tom, my husband and best friend, who made this project a reality through his unconditional love, patience, and wisdom; to my parents, Antonio and Graciela, who have taught me to believe in my dreams; to my children, Frank and Alexandra, who have taught me so much and of whom I am so proud; and to the rest of my family and friends and those who have come into my life for a reason, a season or a lifetime—thanks for also teaching me the art of effective communication.

Cheli

To my husband, Marty, for his love, friendship, loyalty, and all of his great advice; and to all of my family and friends who, throughout my life, have communicated to me that I can do anything I set my mind to. They always have been and always will be my driving force. It is for all of this that I am forever grateful.

Ruth

Table of Contents

The Art of Effective Communication

As I live my life, I understand what it means to communicate.

* ✳ I begin to open myself to change and new ideas.

* ✳ I begin to evaluate my own progress.

* ✳ I begin to allow others to provide constructive criticism.

* ✳ I begin to communicate effectively with everyone.

* ✳ I begin to attend workshops for personal and professional growth.

* ✳ I begin to listen to others.

* ✳ I begin to share ideas and knowledge with others.

* ✳ I begin to be **P**ersuasive.

* ✳ I begin to be **O**bjective.

* ✳ I begin to be **W**ell prepared.

* ✳ I begin to be **E**ffective.

* ✳ I begin to be **R**eflective.

I have P.O.W.E.R.!

How to Use This Book

The snapshots you find throughout this book reflect real-life situations a teacher faces in dealing with parents. While the book follows the typical school-year calendar, divided into month-by-month chapters, the relevant information can be utilized year-round. Common situations, as well as those that are not so common, are presented, followed by strategies, communication tips, and worksheets to support each point. By utilizing these tools you will become:

The checklists help to organize the important information, and the tracking sheets aid in showing parents the progress of their children. Because you will be skillful and confident in presenting important points you want to communicate to parents, you will present yourself as the consummate professional during a face-to-face meeting, phone conference, or Internet contact. By using the worksheets and preparing ahead of time whenever possible, you will find you will have additional time to research any outside source you may want to recommend, such as websites, school personnel, outside agencies, books, magazines, and district personnel.

- Proactive.
- Organized.
- A Good Record-Keeper.
- An Accurate Reporter of Information.

www.School-talk.com

Read the snapshots and tips to gain insight to a problem similar to the one you are facing or about to encounter. Your real-life situations may include elements of multiple snapshots. You can mix and match and adapt them to fit your comfort zone and individual circumstance. Use the tip information and the worksheets, as needed, to guide you through each situation. These keys, tips, and worksheets will assist you in communicating successfully.

Before turning the pages we recommend that as your first step in your journey toward becoming an effective communicator, you take time and do the **Communication Skills Assessment** *(Worksheet #1*, page 140*)*. This will help you to determine your level of comfort when speaking with parents, to recognize your areas of strength, and to notice areas that need some additional assistance. We have also included a **Quarterly Self-Evaluation Checklist** *(Worksheet #2*, page 141*)* to keep you on track and a **Countdown to the First Day of School Checklist** *(Worksheet #3*, page 142*)*.

Our goal, as you read and practice the tips throughout this book, will be to establish a positive working relationship with parents.

My Goals:

1. _____
2. _____
3. _____
4. _____
5. _____
6. _____

Notes :

INTRODUCTION:
A Communication Blueprint for a Great School Year

> "The difference between a smart man and a wise man is that a smart man knows what to say, a wise man knows whether or not to say it."
> **Frank M. Garafola**

Congratulations! By reading this book you are taking the first step toward acquiring those essential skills that will serve you for a lifetime as an effective communicator.

Let's face it—everyone needs to communicate. But effective communication is more than just talking—it encompasses pursuing a deeper understanding, an open sharing of ideas, the willingness to brainstorm without criticizing, and the effective dissemination of information. It means getting to the core of what we are all about. Tact and skill in handling people are enviable traits in any profession, but for the successful teacher, they are essential. *Teacher Talk!* will show you how you can acquire or enhance these skills and then utilize them effectively.

Imagine taking a snapshot of a situation and being able to assess it. In the following pages, you will find fifty-two snapshots that we have captured for you. These snapshot snippets portray situations every teacher may encounter. Accompanying

www.school-talk.com

As an effective communicator, I will be

Persuasive

Objective

Well prepared

Effective

Reflective . . .

I have P.O.W.E.R.!

each snapshot will be strategies you can immediately put to use to direct the outcome of each situation, benefiting both teacher and parent. As you practice these skills and become a better communicator, you will not only acquire a tremendous feeling of personal power, but you will also find parents responding positively to your confidence and ability. By building on this bridge of communication, you will be able to head off potential problems before they arise.

Knowing how to communicate well is the mark of the true teaching professional and can transform a merely competent teacher into a great one. When you follow the techniques offered in the following pages, you will be on your way to succeeding in achieving this goal.

Communication is the genuine exchange of information, ideas, and thoughts whereby an agreement is reached, a schedule is established, a goal is promoted, or a conflict is resolved. By using the techniques in this book, this exchange can become a positive learning and teaching experience.

Notes:

✳ Things to do before the first day:

☐ _____

☐ _____

☐ _____

☐ _____

☐ _____

☐ _____

☐ _____

☐ _____

☐ _____

☐ _____

☐ _____

☐ _____

☐ _____

☐ _____

☐ _____

☐ _____

☐ _____

☐ _____

☐ _____

☐ _____

☐ _____

☐ _____

☐ _____

☐ _____

CHAPTER ONE
September:
First Impressions

> "The trouble with talking too fast is you may say something you haven't thought of yet."
> **Ann Landers**

Overview

You glance at the clock: 8:52 p.m., not quite twelve hours to go before you face them. You are ready, confident, prepared. You set the alarm clock and climb into bed, looking forward to a good night's rest before the big day tomorrow.

A few hours later, your eyes fly open. This time the clock says 2:10 a.m. Try as you might, you can't get back to sleep. The butterfly syndrome has hit, leaving your stomach tied in knots and turning your earlier confidence into apprehension. You know that creating the right first impression is so important for setting the tone for the entire year. But will you succeed in doing so?

Meeting with parents, whether on the first day of school, at an Open House, or in other situations, can be a challenge. In this chapter we will address effective communication techniques for conducting a smooth first day of school, putting on a relaxed Open House, and learning how to master the keys to dealing with parents.

*For a smooth year consider having a Parent Suggestion Box.

www.school-talk.com

The Snapshots:

1. The overzealous parent at Open House.

2. The parent who wants to talk daily just before school.

3. The parent who wants to know what, when, and how you teach.

4. The parent who wants to put his child in another class.

5. The parent who always corners you in the hallway.

Communication is an exchange of information. If you are not engaging in an exchange, you are not communicating.

Snapshot #1:

The Overzealous Parent at Open House

www.school-talk.com

You carefully go over your notes and scan the entire classroom. Everything is in order. You have taken time to plan well, and you are certain this Open House/orientation meeting will go smoothly. At 6:00 p.m. the parents begin to trickle in slowly, and within minutes the classroom is packed. You take one last deep breath, pick up your papers, and begin. Just a few minutes into your presentation, you see a hand go up. A question already? Since you haven't had a chance to fully explain your method and philosophy, you ignore the hand, hoping your remaining remarks will answer the question. The hand does not go down, however, but is accompanied by an insistent voice: "Excuse me, I have a question."

You remain in control, poised and polite, the true professional that you are, but you make the mistake of giving the parent the floor. Once in the spotlight, he launches into a monologue about his child while people shift in their seats, yawn, or give him "the look." You have lost control, and as a result you are wasting the other parents' time. Ultimately, all eyes turn to you. How will you steer the meeting back on course without offending the parent? Another type of overzealous parent is one who constantly interrupts your presentation to inquire specifically about his child, even though your agenda states that this meeting is to give general information about the school, your techniques, and the goals for the school year. How should you handle these interruptions?

Tip A:

You can take back control of the meeting and address the concerns of the overzealous parent with the following remarks:

"I understand you are a very concerned parent. Tonight, however, we are pressed for time and have a lot to cover on the agenda. Let's get together after the meeting tonight and set up a time convenient for both of us when we can talk. I want to be sure we have all the time we need to discuss this issue in full." If other parents share the concern of the overzealous parent, perhaps about an issue such as the introduction of a new program or the lack of textbooks and materials, open up the subsequent meeting to anyone who would like to attend.

Take a consensus of the parents who would like to have another meeting. Announce that you will follow up with when and where the meeting will take place. Make sure that you send out the flyer within twenty-four hours of the Open House meeting with the exact date, time, and agenda. Then go back to your agenda and follow it. Do not under any circumstances be sidetracked again. Instead, respond with "We can address that at the meeting planned for . . ."

Tip B:

Another strategy for regaining control of the meeting could be this response:

"Please look in your Open House Packet. Among the papers is a handout giving my phone number and email address, and detailing my schedule for free time. Please contact me so we can set up a meeting to address your concerns. I welcome the opportunity to discuss common goals and become a proactive team for the success of your child."

Materials that you may include in an Open House Packet are:
- **Letter of Introduction** *(Sample A)*
- **Classroom Rules/Policies**
- **Open House Sign-In Form** *(Worksheet #5)*
- **Emergency Contact Form** *(Worksheet #6)*
- **Parent Request for Conference Form** *(Worksheet #7)*
- **Teacher Request for Conference Form** *(Worksheet #8)*
- **Transportation Information Form** *(Worksheet #9)*
- **Volunteer Sign-Up Letter** *(Sample B)*

Even though several of these forms may have already been sent home, it is important to refer to them and make sure that all parents have them.

Snapshot #2:

The Parent Who Wants to Talk Daily Just Before School

It happens every morning like clockwork. The children have already come into the classroom, the beginning bell is just a couple of minutes away, and . . . there she is at your door: Mrs. Talker. She is pleasant but insistent as she catches your eye and smilingly demands your attention: "This will only take a minute . . ." but, of course, it never does. Always the professional, you give her your attention. By the third day, however, you realize that the one minute has evolved into ten minutes. What do you do?

People don't like to be lectured. They like to be engaged in a discussion.

Tip :

Let Mrs. Talker know that you would like to give her the attention she deserves, but you cannot do so just before the start of school. Give her several options when you can both meet and set a time for the conference.

Snapshot #3:

The Parent Who Wants to Know What, When, and How You Teach

Know your teacher's edition.

Belinda's mom has scheduled a meeting for this afternoon, but she has given you no indication what she wants to talk about. Belinda is doing very well academically and socially, so you don't have a clue as to the topic. At the appointed time Belinda's mom enters your classroom, sits down, and begins to tell you that she feels you need to present your class lessons in a different way and that your curriculum could be improved. What do you do?

Tip:

Listen first. Count to ten and remember you are the professional. DO NOT BECOME DEFENSIVE, even though the parent is questioning your ability.

At the conference have the teacher's editions of the textbooks, the grade-level objectives, and the state standards available. Also have available state and district website addresses where she can go for further information. Copy any of the material and make a packet of information for the parent that addresses her concern or question. Explain how you teach—such as with direct instruction, small groups, and so on—and review the homework policy. Support your choice of techniques with research materials. Many book companies have websites with materials and parent tips to which you may want to refer the parent. Invite the parent to see you in action. She may be surprised to see how well you work with the class. If none of these tactics work, ask an administrator, grade-level chair, or department head to help you with this parent.

Snapshot #4:

The Parent Who Wants to Put His Child in Another Class

www.school-talk.com

After your Open House, as you are saying good-bye and shaking hands with all the visitors, one parent takes you aside and says he does not want his child to be in your class. He is concerned that you will move too slowly for his child and that your groups are functioning at a much lower skill level than his child's capabilities.

Tip:

Assure him that his issues are important, but because you need to spend time with every parent who attended that night, you need to schedule a conference with him.

At the conference, present your books and materials and outline the curriculum goals for the year. Also explain that you will be assessing each student within the first two weeks to determine grade-level placement according to the textbook guidelines. At the time of that testing, you will determine which book provides the best starting point for his child. You can offer to schedule another conference to discuss the results. Suggest that in the meantime he look at the homework assignments and read the **Classroom Newsletter** *(Worksheet #12)* to keep up on all the classroom reviews. Remind him that although textbooks review skills for the first few chapters, the difficulty level of future instruction will increase.

Snapshot #5:

The Parent Who Always Corners You in the Hallway

Speak your words in due time.

www.School-talk.com

You're walking down the hall in the morning, thinking about the things you want to get done before school starts, when you are stopped by a student's parent—again. Mrs. Stopper insists on knowing how her child did the day before—on an exam, in getting along with another student, or with his homework. It is something different every day. She'll then go on to ask about the lunch that day or the dirt she spotted outside the door or why the office staff isn't friendlier to her. The topic doesn't really matter—she just wants to chat. But this is your planning time and you resent the daily intrusion. What should you do?

Tip:

Politely state that this is your planning time and it's very important to have everything ready for the children so the day will run smoothly.

Stress that you always take extra time in planning and preparing so that the children have a great learning day. Assure Mrs. Stopper that you welcome the opportunity to speak with her about her child and her concerns, but that you want to be able to give her your full attention. State that you will be sending home the **Communication to Parents for Setting a Conference Form** *(Worksheet #10),* which shows available meeting times. End the encounter with a genuine comment on how you look forward to working with her.

Notes: _____

_____

_____

_____

_____

_____

_____

_____

_____

✳ Things to do for September:

☐ _____
☐ _____
☐ _____
☐ _____
☐ _____
☐ _____
☐ _____
☐ _____
☐ _____
☐ _____
☐ _____
☐ _____

☐ _____
☐ _____
☐ _____
☐ _____
☐ _____
☐ _____
☐ _____
☐ _____
☐ _____
☐ _____
☐ _____
☐ _____

CHAPTER TWO
October:
Helping Hands

"Education is simply the soul of society as it passes from one generation to another."
G. K. Chesterton

Overview

September has come and gone and you've gotten to know your students and their parents. You have encouraged parental involvement and welcome all the help you can get. But how can you leverage the skills, abilities, motivation levels, and circumstances of every volunteer parent to the benefit of the class as a whole?

This chapter will explore a variety of effective methods for dealing with the different types of parent volunteers. The tips at the end of each snapshot will provide you with practical ways to encourage parental involvement in a positive way.

The Snapshots:

6. The nice parent.

7. The parent who is always involved.

8. The parent who never gets involved.

9. The parent who gossips about a child.

10. The parent who gossips about you, the teacher.

www.school-talk.com

Every year, teachers find they have students who bring with them wonderful, enthusiastic, and supportive parents. As teachers we tend to gravitate to these parents—and probably rely on them a little more than we should.

One classic example is that of the parent whom we'll call Mrs. Nice. She often comes by your classroom to give you a warm smile and ask how you are. Sometimes she tells you that she isn't working that day and offers to stay and help. Maybe she even provides you her work schedule for the week, or tells you to call her anytime at her contact telephone numbers, or offers to buy you any supplies that you need.

You begin to rely on Mrs. Nice and welcome her into your classroom. But as Mrs. Nice becomes more involved, she begins to step over the bounds of what a volunteer should do, such as wanting to grade papers. What should you do?

Snapshot #6:
The Nice Parent

Tip:

This parent is a valuable asset, but needs direction.

Your job as the teacher is to assign her specific tasks or perhaps give her a time slot on the same day each week to help with story time, lead a reading group, facilitate small-group instruction, or work on special projects. Remember to smile and let Mrs. Nice know how much you appreciate everything she does. A "thank you" goes a long way.

If you have several parents who assist you in the classroom on a regular basis, you may want to have an orientation meeting or hand out a sheet outlining volunteer guidelines, including what is expected from the volunteers and how they should handle themselves. The **Volunteer Guidelines Sheet** *(Worksheet #13)* offers some sample guidelines you can use for your volunteers, and when you want to send a note of appreciation, you can use the **Volunteer Thank-You Gram"** *(Worksheet #14)*.

Snapshot #7:

The Parent Who Is Always Involved

r. Worker loves being a volunteer. He comes often, always showing up with a smile on his face, ready, willing, and able to do whatever is needed. Your classroom runs like clockwork, but you worry that he is becoming too much of an asset. He wants to do it all, and he sometimes takes charge when other parents are volunteering in the classroom. You find yourself spending too much time worrying about how to keep all the volunteers busy and happy. It gets to the point where you actually feel relieved when you think he won't show up, but then there he is at your door, letting you know that he has free time and has come to work in your classroom. What are you going to do?

Remember to thank your volunteers.

Tip:

Make it a point to be prepared for the anxious, excited parent who has found time to help.

Invite the parent in and find something for him to do. There is always a student who can use an extra review lesson or one-on-one tutoring, a bulletin board that can be changed, or some organizational task to be done. Maybe the main office or the media center needs some extra help. Work with other teachers in your grade level or department and share the wealth. Let the parent know that he truly is a blessing and that you want to have other teachers benefit from his expertise. Try not to turn anyone away; instead, find a spot where that person can not only help but can also be appreciated for his efforts. Remember, if you decline a volunteer's assistance today, he may not return when you really need the help.

Snapshot #8:

The Parent Who Never Gets Involved

At times, conflict comes about because of the inability to communicate clearly and effectively.

No matter what you send home—an invitation, a request for volunteers, a notification of an event—one child's parents never respond, never participate, never get involved. You are concerned for the student as well as for the parents. How do you approach them with this concern?

Tip:

A voice-to-voice telephone call is a must.

Keep calling until you get the parent; try the work and cell phone numbers written on the **Emergency Contact Form** *(Worksheet #6)*. Invite the student's parents to come into the classroom by asking them, "What is a good time for you to come in to school? I'd like for you to attend our special presentation— something I think you'd like to see." If scheduling is a problem because, for example, the father works from 7:00 a.m. to 7:00 p.m., ask if he can take time to eat lunch with his child or arrive a little later to work so that he can meet with you in the morning. Plan this in advance so that he can inform his boss or make any necessary special arrangements to attend the presentation at school. Sometimes parents can arrange to work during their lunch hour and arrive later to work in order to attend a school morning performance or a parent-teacher meeting.

37

Snapshot #9:

The Parent Who Gossips About a Child

Mrs. Wonderful is the best volunteer in your class. You find her diligent, professional, and competent—until you overhear her telling another parent that a child in your class is failing and may possibly be sent to a special education class, information that is confidential and should not be repeated. What should you do?

> Be tactful. Write a conference script with bullets for each important point and practice it.

Tip:

This is a difficult one. You want the parent to continue to volunteer, yet you cannot allow a parent to gossip about students. And if you tell her not to come in anymore, you not only lose a good worker, it's possible she may gossip about you.

Before you do anything, jot down everything you want to say, developing a script you can follow. You want your tone to be empathetic but firm. You will need to be explicit without being accusing or saying anything that might hurt her feelings. The following is an example of how the conversation might go:

"First, I want to thank you for all you do. Both the students and I appreciate it. You have contributed so much to our learning experience. However, I do need to discuss with you something that I overheard. You were talking about a child in this classroom and his academic progress. As explained in the guidelines I distributed at the orientation meeting, it is essential that everyone working within the classroom treat any information regarding a student as confidential. That means it does not leave the classroom. If you happen to overhear confidential information or if anything concerns you while you are here volunteering, please discuss it with me directly. Because I believe in protecting the privacy of all my kids, please understand that I must ask you to adhere to this rule. If you did talk about one of our students, I'm sure you didn't do so on purpose. However, we must all be sensitive to this issue. If you can't be discreet, I will have no choice but to ask you to stop volunteering in our classroom, and I would hate to do that, as I value your volunteer time and you have helped me greatly. Just remember to treat all children as you would like yours to be treated."

Snapshot #10:

The Parent Who Gossips About You, the Teacher

The parent meeting has finally come to a close at well after 9:00 p.m. Exhausted, you begin to leave the auditorium when you hear someone say your name. You turn to answer, then realize that it wasn't someone talking to you, but about you. You shield your eyes to better see the small group of parents at the back of the auditorium listening intently to a man. He is talking about you, and what he's saying is not complimentary. What do you do?

Negative words are draining. Positive words are uplifting.

Tip:

Parents say things about you all the time, both good and bad. This time you just happened to overhear a negative comment about your teaching skills.

Keep your perspective and maintain confidence in yourself. You are a professional, which means you understand that not every parent will be happy with you all of the time. This is not the time to be confrontational. Ignore the incident and let your good work speak for you. Make a special effort to be congenial with any of the parents you recognized in the group. Just because certain parents were there doesn't necessarily mean they agree with the critic.

Notes:

_____

_____

_____

_____

_____

_____

_____

_____

_____

_____

✳ Things to do for October :

CHAPTER THREE
November:
The Academic Track

> *"You don't understand anything until you learn it more than one way."*
> **Marvin Minsky**

Overview

> ## Inform a parent immediately if a child cannot keep up with the classwork.

As the new year begins, new issues arise. This is the perfect time to carefully evaluate where each child stands with his or her academic progress. In this chapter, situations will be presented to guide you in determining which road to travel scholastically with each student and how to convey this to the parent. You will learn how you can talk to parents about:

The Snapshots:

11. The child who performs below grade level.

12. The gifted child.

13. The child whose grades have dropped dramatically.

14. The child who has a learning disability.

15. The child who comes from a non-English-speaking family.

www.school-talk.com

Snapshot #11:

The Child Who Performs Below Grade Level

O ne of your students, Tim, started off the school year slowly. Now, in reviewing test scores, portfolios, and classwork for each student, you see that Tim has neither improved nor caught on to any of the concepts being taught. Report cards are due to come out soon. What do you do?

Tip :   www.school-talk.com

Call the parent and request a conference to discuss his son's academic progress.

In preparation for the conference, check the vision and hearing tests conducted by the school to make sure they were normal. At the meeting, show examples of the student's work found in the portfolio and relate other signs or incidents that convey his lack of comprehension. Do NOT give an opinion or make a diagnosis that the child has a learning problem; instead, let the parent know you are very concerned that progress is not being made. All children have their own unique skills, talents, and abilities. However, at the beginning of each school year there are certain goals and objectives that must be met for each grade-level. One analogy you can use is that of a race: at the beginning of the school year, all the children start with the same grade-level expectations. Now, at the second-semester mark, the majority of the other children have progressed halfway around the track, while his child is still at the first hurdle. Explain how his child, who has had difficulty with the concepts taught, will find it nearly impossible to move on to the more abstract information due to come in the next few months. Show the parent the textbook, pointing out the coming chapters and the increased difficulty of the information to be learned. The more information and backup documentation you present, the easier it will be for the parent to understand the concerns you have raised. Discuss the vision and hearing tests. Ask that parent if the child has been tested by a vision and hearing specialist. If the answer is yes and all was found to be normal, then you need to have a discussion about what can be done next. You may want to have the special education teacher give input on strategies to use to help the child succeed. Listen for any hints in your discussion—perhaps information about other family members who may have had this problem—and learn how the problem was solved in that instance.

A parent whose child is in your class demands that he be tested for the gifted program. She feels her request is justified because the child is bored with school, never seems to have homework to do, and feels you are not giving him any curriculum challenges. You know the child often does his homework in school, so he has no schoolwork to do at home. He has also begun to exhibit undesirable behavior, thus becoming involved in disruptive situations on a regular basis. What should you do?

Snapshot #12:
The Gifted Child

www.school-talk.com

Tip :

Meet with the parent and discuss the work being done in class. Explain the curriculum and how her child is performing.

Show the portfolio and the rubrics you have required, the skills you plan to cover, the work in the textbook you will assign, and any other materials that you use. If you agree with the parent that the child is doing extremely well, say so, but never use the words "gifted" or "bright." These words may come back to haunt you, as the student's next teacher may not agree with you, especially when the difficulty of the work increases. If, at the end of the conference, you both think that the child may have special talents, call in the school counselor or assistant principal to find out the proper procedure for testing. Never promise a parent something you cannot deliver. Let the expert explain the necessary paperwork and testing procedures.

Snapshot #13:

The Child Whose Grades Have Dropped Dramatically

The day after report cards go home, Mrs. Sanchez calls you, clearly upset. "My child received straight A's on her last report card," she says. "Now it's mostly B's and C's. What is going on? Why didn't you let me know? We need to meet immediately to discuss this. I am sick and tired of the school system failing our children." What do you do?

Tip:

(Elementary): Show her a copy of the Interim Progress Report that you sent home four weeks previous to report cards being sent out.

Have available your grade book and the child's portfolio. Explain the information in them. Discuss what you have witnessed in class. Perhaps the child has missed homework assignments. Listen to the unhappy parent, letting her speak without interruption, then explore ideas to solve the situation together. You might want to share tips on how to study, or how to get organized so all assignments are completed on schedule, or give her websites where she can get practice worksheets for her child. You may also want to use the **Missed Homework Alert Form** (*Worksheet #30*) and the **Academic Communication Checklist** (*Worksheet #22*).

Tip:

(Middle/High): Refer to the Elementary Tip and speak to the student after the grade has slipped two levels, for example, from an A to a C.

Tell the student that you are concerned that the quality of her work has declined. Ask if there is a problem you can help with, or if something else is affecting her study habits. Talk about what she hopes to achieve in life. Typical teens will dream of being a superstar, having lots of money, living in a mansion, and driving an expensive car. Let her know that if she's hoping to be recruited to play a sport, for example, scouts from the top schools will want to see good grades as well as sports skills. You can make the analogy that for every grade that goes down, so does the size of the mansion and luxury car. You may want to use the **Missed Homework Alert Form** (*Worksheet #30*) and the **Academic Communication Checklist** (*Worksheet #22*).

Ms. Specialist comes to you with a concern about Suzanne, who she has noticed is having difficulty writing her name correctly and learning sounds, sight words, and spelling words. She has saved many of Suzanne's papers and examples of work for the portfolio. (See the **Portfolio Checklist—** *Worksheet #31).* She has also begun a **Behavior Record Checklist** *(Sample E)* to document the times Suzanne exhibits trouble staying in her seat or does not complete her assignments. The other children are progressing by the scores on the **Individual Tracking Sheet** *(Worksheet #33),* but Suzanne is struggling. What should you do?

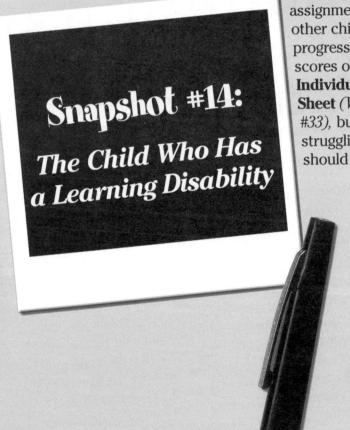

Snapshot #14:
The Child Who Has a Learning Disability

Tip :

Prepare all of your documentation. Make sure that you have all papers and test samples. Call the parent for a meeting.

Send home the **Conference Reminder Form** *(Worksheet #18)* the day before the conference. Use the **Conference Action Plan** *(Worksheet #19)* to prepare for the conference. On the day of the conference, have a school counselor, an administrator, or a special education teacher with you when you discuss your observations with the parent. Listen to the parent and see if she is noticing any of the indicators you have mentioned. Ask if the child has a vision or hearing problem. If not, introduce the idea of psychological testing. Inform the parent that at this point the experts need to assess the child and see what they find. If they find a problem area, they will be able to direct you and the parent so you can create a partnership to educate the child effectively.

Snapshot #15:

The Child Who Comes From a Non-English-Speaking Family

You send a note home for a conference, but the parents do not respond. You send another note home, but still nothing. You then call, but there is no answer and no message machine. Determined to get through to the parents, you try calling at different times. Finally, when you do reach someone, you realize the family does not speak English.

Be aware of when an interpreter may be needed.

Tip :

Always have a list of the children in your class who are Limited English Proficient (LEP) students.

Make a note of these students so that you have it handy whenever you need to communicate with their parent or guardian. Do not assume that because a child speaks English, the parents do also. It is the school's and teacher's responsibility to provide a translator at conferences and to send out important notices in the family's native language. At the conference, stress what you are trying to accomplish and how important it is that the parents be able to assist in educating their child. A recommendation would be to get a close neighbor or family member to help with school projects and homework.

49

Notes: _____

_____

_____

_____

_____

_____

_____

_____

_____

_____

✳ Things to do for November :

☐ _____

☐ _____

☐ _____

☐ _____

☐ _____

☐ _____

☐ _____

☐ _____

☐ _____

☐ _____

☐ _____

☐ _____

☐ _____

☐ _____

☐ _____

☐ _____

☐ _____

☐ _____

☐ _____

☐ _____

☐ _____

☐ _____

☐ _____

☐ _____

☐ _____

☐ _____

CHAPTER FOUR
December: Gearing Up for Winter Break

> "I am always ready to learn although I do not always like being taught."
> Winston Churchill

Overview

Be swift to inform.

As December rolls around, it's not unusual for behavior issues to escalate. While it's the season to be jolly, it's also the time boundaries are often tested. This chapter will deal with certain issues that may escalate during the holiday season. Find ways to keep your sanity as the countdown to holiday recess approaches.

The Snapshots:

16. The tardy child.

17. The truant child.

18. The parent who feels you give too much homework.

19. The parent who wants you to celebrate Christmas.

20. The unkempt child.

21. The child who is a bully in the classroom and on the playground.

www.school-talk.com

One of your students, John, is consistently brought late to school. Not only does he miss the morning drill, but usually at least twenty minutes of instruction. When John finally arrives, the classroom routine is interrupted by the parent's apology and excuses, and you must take time away from the other students to help John get his day started. You realize the parent is having a difficult time at home. What should you do?

Snapshot #16:

The Tardy Child

Have strategies available to present to parents.

Tip:

Tell the parent that you'd like to meet with her to work out a solution to the problem of John's chronic tardiness.

At the meeting, LISTEN to the parent to find out the real reason for John's tardiness. Often the parent simply hasn't figured out the morning routine. You can offer advice on how to get everything done in a timely manner, such as making a chart with morning chores that must be accomplished before the child can watch television, setting the clock ahead by ten minutes, or setting time limits for tasks to be finished by using an alarm clock. You may want to give the parent the **Student School Readiness Task Chart** *(Worksheet #29)*. Other helpful tips include doing some of the necessary tasks the night before, such as laying out clothes, which will eliminate indecision and arguments in the morning; checking all schoolwork and placing it in the backpack; or having lunch made or lunch money put in the backpack. Sometimes a parent needs not only advice, but just someone to talk to. You, the teacher, can help by being sympathetic and offering practical ideas. Sometimes that's all it takes to solve a problem.

For those instances where you are unable to resolve the tardiness problem, find out if the child lives far away from school. Possibly his attending a school closer to home would be a good recommendation.

55

Snapshot #17:
The Truant Child

It's fourth period, and as you take roll, you notice Nicole is absent. One of the students makes a comment under his breath that she is skipping. When you ask the other students if they know where she is, you get mixed responses. Some say they saw her earlier in the day; others say they didn't. What should you do?

www.school-talk.com

Tip:

Immediately contact the office and the parent and let them know that she is not in class.

If you do not have access to a telephone because you are teaching, ask the school counselor or school resource officer to call the parent. Request the students to write a note to you, without signing their names, if they prefer, if they have any information as to where the student might be. By suggesting the students do this anonymously, they will not feel as though they are tattling. You might explain that, for Nicole's safety, it is extremely important for them to let you know where she is. This would not be a snitch.

The following script can be used when calling the parent:

Hello, _____, this is (state your name), Nicole's history teacher. I am calling to let you know that Nicole did not come to my class today. The office has been alerted and we are doing everything we can to find her.

Understandably, the parent may be pretty upset by this news. You may want to ask her to come to the school.

M rs. Skills comes into your classroom without warning, visibly upset. "You are giving out just too much homework," she fumes. "Really, it is just ridiculous what he has to do. I don't have time for it. I work all day and come home late. By the time I feed and bathe him, he has half an hour to do his homework. He has enough school all day. Why does he have to do more? Are you not doing your job? Is that why you have to give out so much homework? Just what is the reason? I'd like an answer!"
What do you do?

Snapshot #18:
The Parent Who Feels You Give Too Much Homework

Do not react to an angry parent; the less said the better.

Tip :

Although you need to address this parent's concern, now is not the time, as she is too upset and you can't leave your class.

Let her know you welcome the opportunity talk with her, but that you cannot do so at the moment. Ask her to leave a telephone number where she can be reached and assure her that you will call to set up a meeting as soon as possible. When you do meet, arrange to have another teacher, the school counselor, or an administrator present. Explain that you assign only enough homework to show parents what the child did in class that day and to help him review concepts covered in class. This keeps the parent informed and helps the student organize his time and create a routine for sharing with the parent what he has learned.

You may suggest the possibility that the child didn't understand what was being taught, so it took him longer than the other children to complete the homework. If this is the case, you may want to sit with the parent and come up with possible reasons why the child is not completing the homework. Come up with a plan that will assist the child in finishing the homework. If the child goes to an after-school program, suggest that the staff work with him on academics and homework. If there is still a problem, offer to work with the parent to create a homework schedule so the activities the child has to do at home get done in a timely fashion and he has free time left before bed.

Snapshot #19:

The Parent Who Wants You to Celebrate Christmas

Celebrate diversity.

Tip :

Schedule a conference with her during which you explain that, because many cultures are represented in the classroom and the school, celebrating just one kind of holiday does not offer the opportunity to honor the celebrations of all the students.

The faculty and staff discussed how to address various holidays and adopted a program that includes and celebrates the many holidays and traditions represented not just by the student body, but of people around the world. Point out that the study of other cultures is also woven throughout all the subjects, allowing for an exciting integration of materials. Invite the parent to come in and share some of her holiday traditions with the children and give suggestions for an art or cooking project. Let her know you are inviting other parents to do the same for their celebrations.

A parent walks into your room and, upon seeing only generic wintertime decorations and no Christmas tree, she launches into a serious talk about the holidays. She feels strongly that you should make the typical Christmas celebration part of your curriculum, especially art. She even volunteers to decorate the room, thinking you may need some help in this area. What should you do?

www.school-talk.com

58

Snapshot #20:
The Unkempt Child

You walk by Charlie's desk and notice an unpleasant smell. A few minutes later, the students around him start holding their noses and making unkind comments. You realize the smell is coming from Charlie. Walking over to talk to him, you notice he is wearing the same clothes he had on the previous day, and they are dirty. Charlie is very embarrassed. What do you do?

Tip :

Ask Charlie to come up to your desk or, if you have someone else who can watch the class, you can address this out in the hall.

Let Charlie know everything will be okay. Quietly ask him why he is wearing the same clothes. Ask him when he last took a bath. If you have a school counselor available, ask him to assist you with this situation. If your school has a clothes/uniform closet, send Charlie to the office to pick up something he can wear instead. Call the child's parents and ask them to come in for a conference. Have the school counselor or nurse involved in this meeting to assist the family with services they may need. Let the parents know that you care about their child and that you are there to help in any way you can.

> **Listen to what the parent has to say. The more you listen, the more the parent will reveal.**

Snapshot #21:

The Child Who Is a Bully in the Classroom and on the Playground

Justin, who is big for his age, likes to pick on the smaller students. You have tried talking to him and have had several conferences with his parents, but he continues to pick on the other children. He does not have many friends, since most of the children are afraid of him. What should you do?

www.school-talk.com

Tip:

First, with the school counselor present, call Justin aside and let him know you will tolerate no more bullying behavior.

Next, contact his parents and set up a conference. Have Justin and the school counselor attend the meeting as well. As a team, create a behavior plan you can use. You may want to use the **Reminder for a Misbehavior Form** *(Worksheet #24)*, the **Behavior Contract** *(Worksheet #21)*, and the **Behavior Observation Chart** *(Worksheet #20)*. On the plan, ask Justin to make suggestions as to how he could improve his own behavior. Have rewards and consequences attached to the plan, making sure Justin is involved in the process. After the plan is put in place, make a point of reporting to the parents any small progress in Justin's behavior. Reinforce positive actions whenever possible. Both parent and child need encouragement and recognition for doing a good job if they are to stay focused and committed to changing the child's behavior.

Time to Reflect:

1. Analyze student data.

2. Assess your midyear classroom goals.

3. Design new strategies to use with students.

4. Read a book and incorporate a new approach in your teaching style.

Notes: _____

_____

_____

_____

_____

_____

_____

_____

_____

✳ Things to do for December:

☐ _____   ☐ _____

☐ _____   ☐ _____

☐ _____   ☐ _____

☐ _____   ☐ _____

☐ _____   ☐ _____

☐ _____   ☐ _____

☐ _____   ☐ _____

☐ _____   ☐ _____

☐ _____   ☐ _____

☐ _____   ☐ _____

☐ _____   ☐ _____

☐ _____   ☐ _____

CHAPTER FIVE

January: Successful Conferencing

"A single conversation with a wise man is better than ten years of study."
Chinese Proverb

Overview

Y ou look at your watch and realize they are ten minutes late. You're not surprised. Up to now the parent conferences have all been routine. But this one will be different. You both dread it and want to get it over.

Can all conferences end successfully even if the subject is sensitive and controversial? The answer is yes, if you have the skills to communicate effectively. In this chapter we will explore various conference snapshots, ranging from the common to the not-so-common, including those that involve sensitive issues.

www.school-talk.com

The Snapshots:

22. The routine conference.

23. The child caught cheating.

24. The child who starts a fire.

25. The parent who sends medication with his child without properly notifying the school.

26. The parent reluctant to administer medication prescribed by the child's doctor.

27. The child caught bragging that she takes and sells drugs.

28. The child caught in a sexual act.

29. A parent who accuses you of yelling.

30. The student who corrects you.

31. The child caught stealing.

Snapshot #22:

The Routine Conference

You are scheduled to meet with a parent who has requested a conference. You're not sure of the topic, as his child is doing well in class. What should you do?

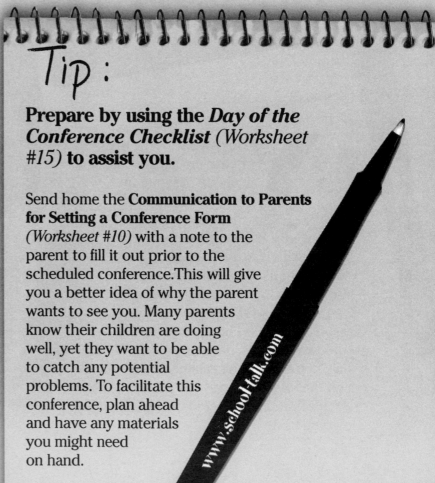

Tip :

Prepare by using the *Day of the Conference Checklist* (*Worksheet #15*) to assist you.

Send home the **Communication to Parents for Setting a Conference Form** (*Worksheet #10*) with a note to the parent to fill it out prior to the scheduled conference. This will give you a better idea of why the parent wants to see you. Many parents know their children are doing well, yet they want to be able to catch any potential problems. To facilitate this conference, plan ahead and have any materials you might need on hand.

Snapshot #23:
The Child Caught Cheating

You call Mr. Extrovert because his son was caught cheating on a test. You request a meeting for the next day to discuss the situation. By the time he arrives, he has already worked himself into an outrage and immediately launches into an angry defense. "My son would never cheat on a test. I questioned him last night and he assured me he would never do that. He knows better, and he certainly hasn't been raised that way. You must be mistaken. I want my child's grade reinstated—now." What are you going to do?

www.school-talk.com

Tip :

Invite the parent to sit down. Let him say what he feels. DO NOT INTERRUPT.

He feels what he has to say is important and wants to be heard. DO NOT become defensive. Be professional and listen intently. When he is finished, say, "Let me tell you what I observed and show you what occurred, since I have the test paper with me." Show the evidence and quietly explain your side of the story and what you saw. Show him everything. You may not change the grade but, as a possible solution, you may want to consider retesting the child on another day. Make the agreement with the parent and the student.

> **Classroom discipline is extremely important. Try always to be aware of every student.**

Snapshot #24:

The Child Who Starts a Fire

ichael and Joseph enter the classroom just before the late bell and sit together in the back. Some of the other students know what has been planned and decide to sit in the back as well. Joseph carefully takes out the bottle of perfume; Michael has his cigarette lighter in his hand and ready. A signal is given and one of the other students distracts the teacher. As Joseph sprays the perfume on a blank piece of notebook paper, Michael lights the lighter and the paper bursts into flames. You notice it immediately and quickly put it out. You make sure everyone is okay. Then what do you do?

Tip:

The first thing you need to do is to get the class under control.

If you are able to call the office for assistance, do so. Since this situation is of a sensitive nature, you want to make sure that you contact the administration immediately and use the **Discipline Referral Form** *(Worksheet #16)*. Set up a conference with each student's parents as soon as possible. Before the meeting, both you and the administration will need to write detailed reports about the event and the actions taken. Reports must also be made to the police and fire departments. Conference with the parents separately; include their children and a representative of the administration. Follow the school's procedures and/or guidelines for handling such an offense. Keep the students involved in this incident apart until the conference; ask each to write a detailed summary of the events. Discuss with the parents all the consequences. Address what will be expected from all the people involved and create a schedule for following up on students, if that is appropriate. If there was damage done to the school or school property, the administration may want to seek restitution from the students or their parents.

You may encounter a parent who denies that his child was involved in the incident. If this is the case, maintain your objectivity and a professional demeanor. Don't get into a debate; simply present the facts. This often will convince the parent that you have assessed the situation correctly. If you don't have any concrete evidence to support your claim, state your case based on the facts that you have. Always be fair and objective in presenting the situation. Any consequences should be handed out fairly and appropriately to all of the parties involved.

As the teacher, you also need to make some decisions about the situation and then voice these to the administration. You may want the students to be placed in separate classrooms or permanently removed from your class.

A student brings medication with her to school. The bottle has been sealed in a plastic bag by the parent and the label clearly shows that it was prescribed for that child and gives instructions on the frequency and amounts of doses to be administered. The child begins to cough horribly. What do you do?

Snapshot #25:

The Parent Who Sends Medication With His Child Without Properly Notifying the School

Medical forms must be on file.

Tip:

Call the parent and explain that no one at the school can administer any medication to any child without an authorized, signed consent form.

Let the parent know also that the child's cough is severe and that you are concerned. Advise him that you will be sending the child to the office/clinic, and that you will ask school personnel to put the form to be filled out in the child's backpack. Once this is on file, designated/official staff will be able to administer the medication. Explain to the parent that this regulation is in place to protect his child and that the school cannot, under any circumstances, administer medicine without this form. You may want to send home the **Guidelines for Medication Letter** *(Sample C).*

At the Open House, talk about what should be done when a child is ill.

If the child needs medication, a form must be on file at the school that gives permission for school personnel to administer medicine. All of the child's medical and emergency information must be up to date. Have copies of the medication approval form and medical information forms handy. Pass them out, ask that they be returned by a certain date, and have a checklist you can consult to make sure all parents have complied.

Snapshot #26:

The Parent Who Forgets to Administer Medication Prescribed by the Child's Doctor

The book hit the floor with such force that it startled the entire class. Everyone looked in the direction of Joe, who had been having a difficult time all day. You are aware that Joe suffers from hyperactivity and have worked with Joe and his parents to make the classroom environment one that works for both Joe and his classmates. Up to now you have been pleased with the progress Joe has made. However, today you notice that Joe is finding it difficult to stay focused and will not remain in his assigned seat. When Joe slams the book on the floor, you approach him and see that the child is very angry. When you ask Joe what is wrong, he replies, "I need my medicine. My mom didn't give it to me today." You immediately become alarmed about the potential danger Joe poses, physically and emotionally, to himself, to you, and to others in the room. Compounding the problem is the reaction of one of the parents volunteering that day. She complains loudly that Joe is out of control and should not be in the classroom with her child. What should you do?

Protect the child's privacy at all times.

Tip :

You have two situations here to be addressed as soon as possible.

Communicate to the parent who witnessed the inappropriate behavior, without revealing any confidential information, that the school is working to remedy the situation. Emphasize your appreciation and concern and promise that you will do everything possible to help the child with the behavior issues and ensure everyone's safety, including that of her child. Next, meet with the parent of the child who is on medication. Have several staff members present, including an administrator. Discuss the behavioral observations and anecdotal records you have been keeping *(Worksheets #25, #26, #27, and #28)*. Mention specific patterns you have noticed, such as that the child was acting up in the afternoon or that the medication was consistently ineffective. If the parent is forgetting to give the child the medication, you may want to suggest to have the medication given at the school. School personnel are trained to administer medication throughout the day as needed. Before this is done, the parent needs to give signed consent and contact the child's medical doctor for a signed form stating the medication's name and dosage and how often it needs to be taken. A medication log is completed on each child every time medication is given.

Before speaking with an expert, confirm that he has the password the parent has given to you to use. This will ensure that you are speaking to the correct person and will protect the confidentiality between all parties.

Snapshot #27:

The Child Caught Bragging That She Takes and Sells Drugs

Susan goes into the empty restroom and chooses to use the stall at the far end. As soon as she closes the door, three girls come into the bathroom, talking and laughing. Apparently thinking they are alone, one brags that she's tried heroin and can get it from her older brother. Susan recognizes the voice of the girl and becomes scared, uncomfortable, and not sure what to do. She finally comes to you, her favorite teacher, and tells you the story. What should you do?

www.school-talk.com

Tip :

Let the child who comes to you know that she did the right thing and assure her you will maintain her confidentiality.

You can explain to the child that this is known as "a good tattle" and you respect her courage and maturity. Take the matter to the administration and the school counselor. In many schools, there are procedures in place for these types of situations. If, for some reason, your school does not have procedures, make a recommendation to the counselor and school principal to develop some. You may want to suggest that the school counselor come into your room to discuss the dangers of drugs.

Make sure your school has procedures in place where students and staff can anonymously report serious incidents.

Snapshot #28:

The Child Caught in a Sexual Act

A: You notice several children kissing and hugging in the halls.

B: A parent observes students behind the school not just kissing, but engaging in more explicit sexual behavior, and reports it to you. What should you do?

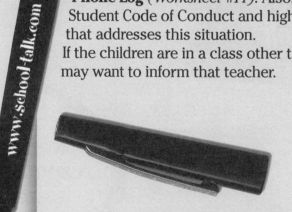

Tip:

In both cases, report the activities to the administration and the school counselor.

Where a parent is involved, assure him that you appreciate his telling you and that you will take the matter to the administration and together you will work out a resolution.

If the participants are your students, contact the parents and inform them of the situation that took place. Make sure that you fill out a **Parent/Teacher Phone Log** *(Worksheet #11)*. Also, send home the Student Code of Conduct and highlight the area that addresses this situation.

If the children are in a class other than yours, you may want to inform that teacher.

73

A parent comes to you and complains that you yell too much at her son. She blames you for his inability to learn because her son says all you do is scream. You listen attentively. Explain to the parent that you do not yell but speak in a normal tone of voice to refocus his attention. Her son consistently does not listen, does not perform the task when first asked, and doesn't stay on task. Sometime later, the parent comes in again, this time complaining that her child hates school because all you do is pick on him. After talking with her and listening carefully, you learn that the child is the same way at home. This parent does not know how to handle the problem and is expecting you, the professional, to fix it. What do you do?

Snapshot #29:

A Parent Who Accuses You of Yelling

Tip :

Talk with her and suggest you work as a team to effect positive changes in the child's behavior.

Come up with a plan that will support both of you in doing so. Decide what goal you want to accomplish first: paying attention, performing a task when first asked, or staying focused. Come up with specific actions the child is to take. At school it could be to take out his homework journal/planner, pencil, and homework as soon as he gets into class. At home it could be to do homework as soon as he gets home. Ask the parent for her input and create the plan together. Next, track his progress by using the **Work Habits Anecdotal Checklist** *(Worksheet #25 or #26)*. Establish a system of rewards and consequences for the student's behavior. The chart will make it clear to all parties how to carry out the plan. Suggest a follow-up meeting to assess and refine the chart as needed.

Be slow to anger. Recognize that you are responsible for your actions and must act in a responsible way.

Snapshot #30:

The Student Who Corrects You

As you are delivering your lecture in social studies theory, you misspeak and say "exploration" instead of "annexation." A student yells out that you made a mistake and laughs, clearly mocking you and being disrespectful. You ask him to stop and he refuses. What should you do?

Tip:

www.school-talk.com

If this is an elementary school child:

You may be able to handle it in the classroom. You can try the following: Finish the discussion and give the other students the follow-up activity to complete. Then pull the disrespectful student aside and speak to him about how he felt and how his response to your mistake could have been approached in a better, more constructive way. Encourage him to discuss with you workable solutions. One possibility is to raise his hand instead of calling out. Create a document in a contract form that incorporates the suggestions you and he came up with. Sign it, ask him to sign it, and then send it home for his parent to read and sign. You may want to use the **Behavior Contract** *(Worksheet #21)* and the **Student Behavioral Insight Form** *(Worksheet #23)*. If he acts this way again, remind him of the rules you jointly agreed upon. This contract should be easily accessible so the child can read it the next time he acts inappropriately and then self-correct his behavior.

If this is a middle school or high school child:

Contact the administration immediately to have the child removed from your classroom and taken to the office to be dealt with by the administration. A conference should be held with you, the student, the parent, and a representative from the administration. Use the **Behavior Contract** *(Worksheet #21)* and the **Student Behavioral Insight Form** *(Worksheet #23)* to begin a behavior plan so that the behavior doesn't occur again. Remember, as the teacher, you must decide what action will work best, given the student and the situation. This is a control issue, and it is important that you show that you have control of the class and your emotions.

When contacting a parent, if you have no choice but to leave a message, do not explain the problem in the message. Ask the parent to return your call as soon as possible. Do not forget to mention that the child is all right, but that you would like to talk with him as soon as possible about a behavior incident. Leave all the contact information again, as the parent may not be at home when you call. Also, make sure that the parent signs all conference documentation. Always document all conferences, even if it is an unplanned telephone conference. Make sure you put the telephone conference and the outcome on your **Parent/Teacher Phone Log** *(Worksheet #11)*.

75

Snapshot #31:

The Child Caught Stealing

You brought your cell phone to school and put it in the top drawer of your desk. Shortly thereafter, when you open the drawer, you see that it's missing. No one has left the room since the cell phone was last seen. You immediately address the situation with a discussion about stealing and breaking the law. As you circulate the room, you notice that the cell phone is sticking out of a student's desk. You take the cell phone back and state that you will be contacting his parents. When contact is made, the parent is extremely irate. What should you do?

> **Be slow to speak. Make sure what comes out of your mouth is what you intended to say. Words once spoken cannot be taken back.**

Tip :

A: Try to find students who witnessed the act and begin to conduct an investigation. An administrator should be present.

The students can write down their account. You may want to use the **Incident Communication Report** *(Worksheet #17)* to write down a description of the incident and how it is being handled. When the parent comes in, have the administrator remain. A third party present may help defuse the confrontation. Let the parent speak freely. Do not interrupt him until he feels he has had his chance to say everything he is feeling. If you do try to say something while he is still angry, the situation may get out of control. Once he is finished, you may want to tell him what you observed. You then need to call his child in and discuss the situation that occurred in class. Now all the parties can have a dialogue and the administration can determine what course of action needs to be taken. The Student Code of Conduct may address the action that must be taken for this misbehavior.

Not all conferences work.

Tip:

B: When a conference doesn't work because the parent is too angry to engage in a reasonable discussion, don't keep repeating yourself or get caught in a verbal confrontation. Instead, be mindful of the situation and focus on listening.

Acknowledge the parent's opinion. Allow for differences. Try to continue the discussion in a calm and objective manner. If this is not possible, consider ending the meeting and ask the parent if you can reschedule for a later date. Sometimes extending a conference that has become emotionally charged can irrevocably shatter any chance of maintaining effective communication with the parent. Come to an agreement with the parent that at a follow-up conference, each one of you will bring a written list of issues and suggestions on how you wish to address them.

*Pupil Portfolio:

P Prepare one for each pupil; Papers that are dated; Precise with corrections; and Placed in a folder.

O Organize the portfolios and place the most current sample of work on the top.

R Rubrics are available for all major projects and ready for review in the portfolio.

T Tracking the student's progress throughout the year is the ultimate goal.

F Follow-up meeting is important to the portfolio communication process with parents.

O Open to suggestions and criticisms while sharing the portfolio work samples with parents.

L Listen at least fifty percent of the time.

I Introduce innovative education plans and set individual goals at the conference after carefully examining the individual student's portfolio.

O Offer concrete suggestions and guidelines, summarize main points, and duplicate the conference form with signatures to file as a student record.

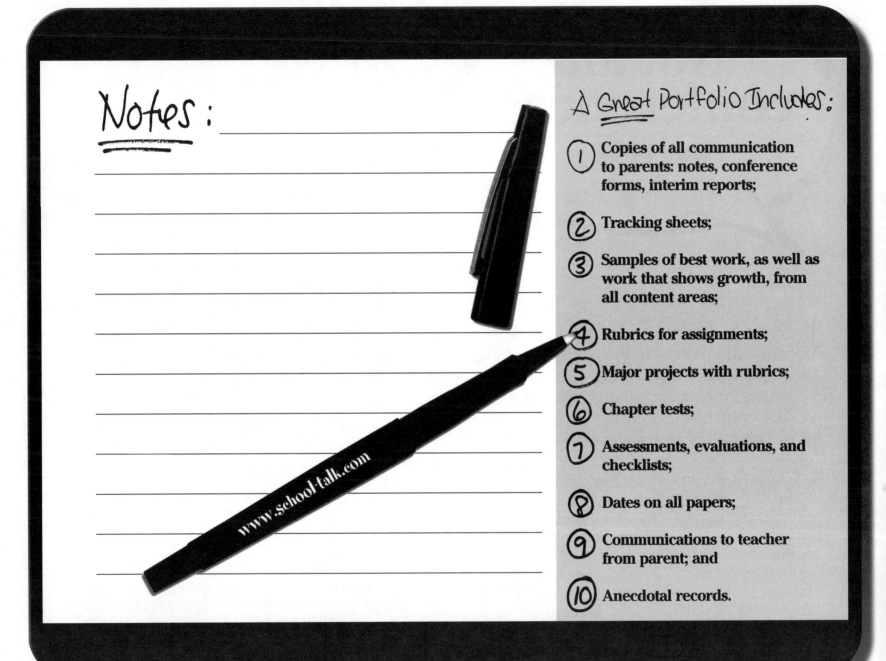

Notes: _____

A Great Portfolio Includes:

1. Copies of all communication to parents: notes, conference forms, interim reports;

2. Tracking sheets;

3. Samples of best work, as well as work that shows growth, from all content areas;

4. Rubrics for assignments;

5. Major projects with rubrics;

6. Chapter tests;

7. Assessments, evaluations, and checklists;

8. Dates on all papers;

9. Communications to teacher from parent; and

10. Anecdotal records.

www.school-talk.com

* Things to do for January:

☐ _____
☐ _____
☐ _____
☐ _____
☐ _____
☐ _____
☐ _____
☐ _____
☐ _____
☐ _____
☐ _____

☐ _____
☐ _____
☐ _____
☐ _____
☐ _____
☐ _____
☐ _____
☐ _____
☐ _____
☐ _____
☐ _____

CHAPTER SIX
February:
Measuring Up

"Learning is like rowing upstream: not to advance is to drop back."
Chinese Proverb

Overview

This chapter will address how to explain to a parent the different types of tests and the importance of multiple assessments in creating an accurate profile of each student. Different ways to communicate the importance of testing for each student are also explored. In the following pages, you will learn how to respond when:

The Snapshots:

32. The parent complains, "Standardized testing is ruining my child."

33. The parent doesn't understand the test scores.

34. The parent asks, "Why do you give weekly spelling tests?"

35. The parent feels his child becomes too stressed over testing.

36. The parent wants to know in what other ways you can assess her child.

www.school-talk.com

A parent comes in because she is concerned about her child's scores on the standardized test. Her child has always been an A student, but this level of achievement is not reflected on the standardized test scores. What do you do?

Snapshot #32:

The Parent Complains, "Standardized Testing Is Ruining My Child."

Tip :

At a conference with the parent, share any information you have on the tests, such as handouts prepared by the state that explain the test scores and how the parent should interpret them.

Make it as simple as you can. You can also share addresses to websites that have a line-by-line explanation. Second, talk about the student and the test situation. Because this was a timed test, perhaps he may have felt pressured; or perhaps because the test was given in February and not at the end of the year, there may have been questions concerning material not yet covered in class. You may also address how you determine grades for the report card, which takes into consideration not just aptitude, but attitude, classwork, participation in class discussions, reports, and homework completion, which all are ingredients used for a report card grade.

Snapshot #33:
The Parent Doesn't Understand the Test Scores

Tip:

All testing companies send an information manual that explains the test and testing scores.

As the education professional, you must use this information to become the expert on interpreting the tests. Use the **Standardized Test Explanations Form** *(Worksheet #35)* to assist you. Once you feel confident that you can explain the testing system, respond to concerned parents by setting up a conference. At the meeting, use the sample test, tracking sheet, and test scores provided by the testing company to explain the scores. You may also want to use the breakdown of how your class did as a whole, as well as what each student achieved, by using the **Class Tracking Sheet** *(Worksheet #34)*. Give the parent an opportunity to respond to the information, so you can be sure he understands what you are saying before you move on.

Explain to the parent the areas in which his child did well and those in which the child may need additional help. This information can help the parent work with the child during the summer so that she comes better prepared for school in the fall.

> **Know how to interpret the test scores. Include a chart or letter explaining the scoring when handing out the test results.**

Standardized testing is finally over and everyone on staff breathes a sigh of relief. The reprieve turns out to be brief, however, when the tests come back and the scores are sent home. Many of the parents are confused about the scores. One such parent is Mr. Concerned, who drops by your class full of questions: "I don't understand this grading system. What do all of these numbers mean? Did my child pass? Did she do better than last year? Does a six on this line mean she did badly?" What do you do?

Snapshot #34:

The Parent Asks, "Why Do You Give Weekly Spelling Tests?"

Know how to justify your tests.

Mrs. Bee comes to see you, asking, "Why does my child have to memorize these spelling words every week? It's become torture to force him to sit down every Thursday night and study them. I see absolutely no purpose in it. He hates it and so do I. His report card shows that he can't do it and I don't think that it's fair." What do you do?

Tip :

Arrange to have a conference with the parent, as there may be more to this story than you think.

Because the child is having difficulty with this assignment, the parent may become frustrated as well. Many times parents resent having to take time out of their busy schedules to help children study for tests, so you must be able to explain why this part of your curriculum is important to the child. Try to find out why it is so tedious for the child. You may discover that the child is having difficulty working with the fifteen assigned words; you could suggest starting with ten words, then building upon the success of ten by increasing the number to twelve and then fifteen. This will develop the child's self-confidence and decrease the parent's frustration. Take a look at the scores. It may be that the words are too difficult for the child, who may be incorrectly placed and should move to a lower skills group. You can also suggest that the child start studying for the spelling test on Monday and tackle a little bit every night instead of cramming for the test the night before. Your best justification for testing is to know the educational reasons for doing the testing. It may be to build self-confidence, to increase sight word recognition, to review phonetic concepts, and/or to review words in the current literature selection or the news. Testing can also help a student learn how to memorize facts, increase vocabulary, and develop other study skills.

Snapshot #35:
The Parent Feels His Child Becomes Too Stressed Over Testing

A parent calls you, concerned that while his child is an A student, she never does well on standardized tests. You know she works very hard to achieve top grades, stays focused, and has good time-management skills, yet her test scores are consistently low. The parent wants to know if he should do something to help her, such as hire a tutor. He's particularly anxious for her to do well on the tests you give, as poor test scores may keep her from being placed in the advanced classes, especially if she attends a different school next year. What do you do?

Tip :

Schedule a meeting with the parent. Have an outline of ideas both you and the parent can use to help the child.

You may suggest sending the student to the reading specialist, who may have some test-taking tips or be able to recommend books on the subject. You can promise to go over some test-taking strategies in class, which would benefit all the students, and you can offer to speak with the child before school or during a planning period to help ease her anxiety. At home, the parent may want to give practice tests from workbooks, which can be purchased at any discount store; he can also go online to find practice tests. When administering the test, the parent should set a timer so the student becomes accustomed to the timed test and

learns how to strategize. Inform the parent you will make sure all major exams will be posted on the homework journal/daily planner, so that both parent and student will know when the test is coming. This can also be done on a blank monthly calendar, which allows the child and parent to see the tentative schedule for the month at a glance. This will help with time management in studying for the exam. Advise the parent to check in with you to make sure that the test date has not been changed, as a result of moving through the chapter more quickly or slowly than expected.

Another idea for the parent is to play study games or use flash cards. A good time for this is during the ride to and from school. Have the child become the teacher and quiz the parent. The parent can give rewards for study time well spent. The teacher should also remember to praise the student whenever possible, and to let the parent know when the positive turnaround occurs.

Snapshot #36:

The Parent Wants to Know in What Other Ways You Can Assess Her Child

A parent comes into her conference very concerned that her child does not seem to be doing very well on some of the tests. She is afraid her child will not be promoted even though she can do most of the work. She emphasizes that her child gets very nervous when she has to take a test and does not sleep well the night before. The parent asks if there is some other way you can assess her child's level of academic achievement other than by testing. What do you do?

A multi-assessment program gives the most complete picture of a student's performance.

Tip:

Assure the parent that you understand the situation; tell her some children do not test well.

Make it clear that you know a chapter test does not give the full picture. Explain that you have many ways of determining a student's level of skill and knowledge. Through portfolios, homework, and small-group instruction, you are well aware of her child's strengths and weaknesses. You can show her your grade book (only her child's grades should be visible). Show how the portfolio uses dated samples to chart and help spotlight what areas still need to be reviewed or taught again using another modality. Review test samples, classwork samples, group projects, and rubrics for oral presentations and writings, all of which combine to give you the true profile of each student in your classroom.

www.school-talk.com

Notes: _____

_____

_____

_____

_____

_____

_____

_____

_____

_____

* Things to do for February:

CHAPTER SEVEN
March:
The "Extras" of the "Extracurricular"

"Education is the ability to listen to almost anything without losing your temper or your self-confidence."
Robert Frost

Overview

Teachers must learn to deal with situations both inside and outside the classroom. This balance is essential to create healthy and happy individuals who will succeed in school and carry this success throughout their lives. This chapter will present situations involving some of these extras that encompass student participation in sports, clubs, student elections, and field trips. Learn how to talk to the parent when:

www.school-talk.com

The Snapshots:

37. The child is ineligible to play in a sport, even though he is the star athlete.

38. A child is preparing to go on a field trip when you find head lice.

39. The parent challenges the votes for the student council elections.

40. The child can't afford to go on a field trip.

41. There are too many chaperones for a class field trip.

Snapshot #37:

The Child Is Ineligible to Play in a Sport Even Though He Is the Star Athlete

Y ou have noticed that a student's grades have dropped well below the standards set by the coach/school system to play on the football team. You inform the coach that because of his poor grades, the child can no longer be on the team. It's your job to call the parent. When you make the call, an answering machine picks up. Not wanting to delay this time-sensitive news, you go ahead and leave a message with full details. First thing the next morning, the parent storms into your room very upset. What do you do?

Never leave a message on voice mail or an answering machine that may cause distress to the student or parent.

Tip : **First and foremost, you do not want to leave a message that is negative or potentially distressing to the parent or child on a machine, as such news may create an even more difficult situation.**

Because you can see the parent is very upset, find someone to cover your room for a few minutes so you can resolve the situation immediately. Find a quiet, private spot to sit down and show the parent the team's code of conduct and qualifications. Highlight the area that describes the minimum grade point average each student must maintain to be a member of the team. Go on to show the parent your grade book, explaining why you gave his child the grades you did. You may offer the option that if the student's grades improve, the coach may reinstate him. If possible, try to find out why the student's grades are dropping. Ask whether the concepts are becoming more difficult, if the student is watching too much television, or whether he is engaging in too many other activities that don't leave enough time for studies. Once you discover the WHY for the drop in academic achievement, you can offer suggestions to remedy the problem. Recommend using the **Improving Study Habits Checklist** *(Sample G)*, trying better time management, or developing a "positive change" jar. This jar would have a card that a student would get upon improved behavior. On the card would be a special message just for that child. If it fits your schedule, you may want to offer to tutor the student on a limited basis. In this way, you can assist in making a positive change.

93

Snapshot #38:

A Child Is Preparing to Go on a Field Trip When You Find Head Lice

It's 8:30 a.m. and you are preparing to go on a field trip. A child is sitting at her desk scratching and scratching her head. You walk by and notice that she may need to be examined for head lice. The child is examined and lice are detected on her scalp. The secretary notifies the parent and asks her to pick up the child. The child does not go on the field trip. The parent comes into your class the next day, yelling, "My daughter came home crying yesterday because you told her she had lice and wasn't able to go on the field trip. You also said that our house is dirty. You should never have said that. For your information, our house is very clean and she does not have lice. If you had concerns, why didn't you call or write a letter about this? I think the way you handled this was terrible!" What do you do?

Send a notification letter home immediately when there is a lice outbreak in your classroom.

Tip:

Anytime you find lice, let the administration know so they can conduct a lice check throughout the school. Arrange a conference with the parent of the child in question.

Review the standard head lice letter posted on your communication bulletin board, along with any other information you've sent home. Explain that the only way to make sure that the lice do not spread is to examine each child, determine who has been infected, give full instructions on how to get rid of them, and follow up the treatment ten days to two weeks later. Convey that you regret that the child was not able to attend the field trip. Inform the parent in clear terms that you did not tell the child or anyone else that her house was dirty and that was how the child got lice. Explain that an infestation of lice is no reflection on a child's hygiene. Perhaps the child misinterpreted a statement made during a mini-presentation in your classroom. Apologize if you were mistaken in your identification of lice in her child, but that you must err on the side of caution. Show her what you thought were indications of lice in her child's hair and give her a demonstration of how to identify it.

Snapshot #39:

The Parent Challenges the Votes for the Student Council Elections

Tip:

Set up a meeting with the parent, assuring her you want to take care of this as soon as possible.

Have the procedures for voting available for the parent to review. Also have any other teacher or staff person who assisted you in the election and an administrator, or their designee, at the meeting. Explain to Mrs. Overachiever how the voting was done and that proper procedures were followed. Express your regret that her child didn't make student council president. If she demands to see the ballots, have them available for her review.

Mrs. Overachiever calls you, very distressed over the results of the recent student council election. She is sure that her child, who had been running for student council president, lost, but should have won. She alleges that the election must have been rigged somehow and demands the election be done again. What do you do?

Always keep ballots cast in an election locked up and in a safe place for one year in case any challenges arise after the election.

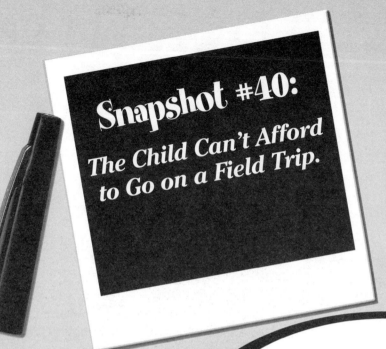

Snapshot #40:
The Child Can't Afford to Go on a Field Trip.

Tip:

Check the telephone log and parent contact sheet to make sure that all telephone numbers are current.

Ask the child if there are any new telephone numbers to try. Check with the school secretary to see whether the school has some kind of provision for paying for needy students. The parent organization may have funds designated to cover such instances. If money is available, call the parent and tell her the school has scholarships for children who qualify, and you would like Joey to use this resource. Make a point of saying how you are looking forward to having Joey participate. You may want to mention that you have even assigned her child a special job, such as bus monitor. Mention that you use the buddy system on field trips, and Joey's best friend, Johnny, would feel better having her son there to be his partner. Try to convey that this is a common situation and that there's no need for her son to miss the trip. Perhaps emphasizing that you would personally like her son to attend will be the persuasive factor.

The school is planning a field trip that includes admission to an attraction and lunch. Many of the students are bringing spending money as well. All of the parents have sent in the required amount except for Joey's. You send home a note, and then call and leave a message, but the parent doesn't respond to any of your reminders. You ask Joey if his parents have sent in the money. He replies, "Mommy has no money." What do you do?

Be compassionate.

Snapshot #41:

There Are Too Many Chaperones for a Class Field Trip

For your upcoming class field trip, you asked in your newsletter if any parents would like to volunteer as chaperones. More than enough parents responded, both on your email and on the trip slip reminder, many of which came in on the same day. A dilemma to solve, but a nice one for a change. What do you do?

Tip:

Carefully read all the responses.

Try to choose those parents who have not had an opportunity to chaperone before or those who you know would really appreciate coming and, perhaps, could not afford to without being a chaperone. Once you've selected and notified the chaperones, call the other parents. Don't leave a message, but persist until you get the parent in person. Explain that you had more volunteers than you anticipated and that you won't be able to offer them a spot this time. If they are willing to drive on their own, maybe carpooling with another parent, and to pay their own way into the attraction, you would love to have them come along. If they are not open to that suggestion, invite them to come on the next trip, letting them know you'll put them at the top of the list.

Thank parents in advance for their willingness to act as chaperones.

Notes: _____

_____

_____

_____

_____

_____

_____

_____

_____

_____

* Things to do for March:

- [ ] _____
- [ ] _____
- [ ] _____
- [ ] _____
- [ ] _____
- [ ] _____
- [ ] _____
- [ ] _____
- [ ] _____
- [ ] _____
- [ ] _____
- [ ] _____
- [ ] _____

- [ ] _____
- [ ] _____
- [ ] _____
- [ ] _____
- [ ] _____
- [ ] _____
- [ ] _____
- [ ] _____
- [ ] _____
- [ ] _____
- [ ] _____
- [ ] _____
- [ ] _____

CHAPTER EIGHT
April: Making the Grade

"The most important thing in communication is hearing what isn't being said."
Author Unknown

Overview

This chapter will deal with those issues surrounding grades. Parents often question how and why a teacher awards a particular grade. The teacher must learn how to articulate his personal ideology, as well as the school's philosophy, on determining an appropriate grade, which includes not just academic performance, but also effort and conduct. You will learn how to talk to parents when:

The Snapshots:

42. A child needs to be retained.

43. The parent questions the grade you have given her child on a report card, test, or project.

44. The parent mistakenly believes her child to be gifted, which creates stress for the child.

45. The parent is in denial about his child's exceptionality, fearing the stigma of a negative label.

46. The parent wants her child to skip a grade.

Snapshot #42:
A Child Needs to Be Retained

The guidelines for retention of a student have just come out and you can see that one of your students may fit the criteria. You call the parents immediately to inform them that with the skills their child is exhibiting in reading, he may have to repeat the same grade. What else do you do?

> **Document, document, document.**

Tip:

Schedule a conference to explore the situation more thoroughly with the parents.

Let them know at the onset that the rules for retention are set down by the state, the school board, or the school administration. You have no choice but to comply with these standards and guidelines. Always document the child's progress through paperwork, samples of work, and any conferences with the parent. Use the **Conference Action Plan** *(Worksheet #19)* as a guide to use in a conference. Keep all information for documentation in a locked file cabinet, as these files are confidential and must not be misplaced. Go over the criteria for retention with the parents and document that you discussed this possibility prior to the end of the year. Use the **Retention Warning Letter** *(Sample M)* as a guide. You may also want to have the grade-level chair, school counselor, or an administrator at this meeting to assist you. Always be prepared to give parents information about all options for help and assistance for the student.

Snapshot #43:
The Parent Questions the Grade You Have Given Her Child on a Report Card, Test, or Project

A parent drops into your room after report cards are distributed and challenges how you determined her child's grade in social studies. She shows you all the test scores and letter grades her child has received, and she calculates that the grade should be a B, not the C you gave. She knows the child is working hard and doesn't understand the discrepancy. What do you do?

Keep accurate and complete records.

Tip :

Ask the parent to schedule a conference to discuss the issue. At the meeting, you want to be able to document how you have determined a grade or a score.

Rubrics are the best answer for this because they demonstrate what comprises your grading system, such as test scores, level of effort, homework completion, written and oral reports, and class participation. Inform the parent that you generally give students another opportunity with sufficient time to complete the project. The idea is not to have a child fail, but to succeed. Also show the parent your grade book (only showing their child's grades). It may indicate that the child missed one of the assignments that would have been averaged into her grade. Share the work in the child's portfolio with the parent. Make sure to include all rubric grades just in case one paper may not have made it home for her to see.

Snapshot #44:

The Parent Mistakenly Believes Her Child to Be Gifted, Which Creates Stress for the Child

Don't diagnose or label students; leave it to the appropriate professionals.

A parent comes in daily to tell you her son is bored and you are not challenging him enough with your curriculum. "The work is too easy. He's obviously a child prodigy—he always gets straight A's," states the parent. "You send me notes that his behavior is getting worse, but it's because you are not challenging him. I just don't understand why you won't get him labeled as gifted." What do you do?

Tip:

Set up a formal conference with the parent.

Send home the **Conference Reminder Form** *(Worksheet #18)* several days before the conference. Show the portfolio and the books the student is using. Use the **Portfolio Checklist** *(Worksheet #31)*. Discuss how you feel he is doing. Assess the situation, remaining open to the possibility that the parent may be right. Agree to give the student an end-of-level test to see how he does. Tell her that if he does well, you will move him to the next book. If you do not use that level, find a teacher on your team who does. Let the parent know that if her son continues to excel, you can meet again in three to four weeks. Set the date for that conference so the parent knows you are committed to monitoring her son's progress. Inform the parent that if her son is still going through the work quickly and getting straight A's, you will set up a meeting with the assistant principal to discuss whether she feels testing the student for the gifted designation is appropriate. A word of caution: Stay away from using such words as "bright" or "exceptional" to describe a student. Sometimes a child, especially in the lower grades, can do extremely well, but in later grades, when the work changes from a concrete to an abstract level of thinking, that same student may function more at his grade level. If you label him incorrectly as gifted, the next teacher may not find this to be true, creating a difficult situation for the next teacher. Let the appropriate professionals determine any labels.

105

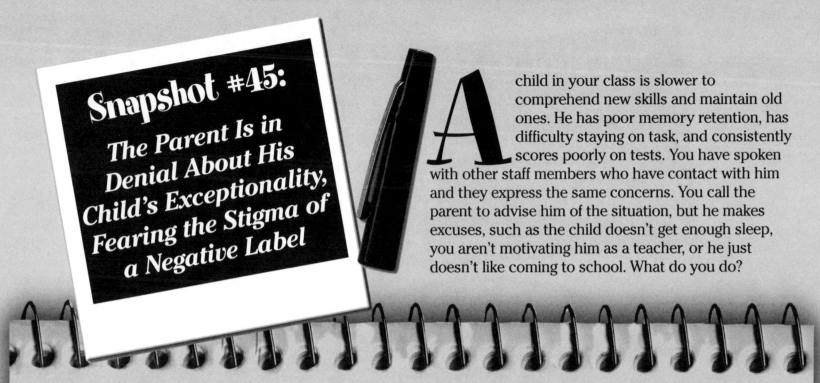

Snapshot #45:
The Parent Is in Denial About His Child's Exceptionality, Fearing the Stigma of a Negative Label

A child in your class is slower to comprehend new skills and maintain old ones. He has poor memory retention, has difficulty staying on task, and consistently scores poorly on tests. You have spoken with other staff members who have contact with him and they express the same concerns. You call the parent to advise him of the situation, but he makes excuses, such as the child doesn't get enough sleep, you aren't motivating him as a teacher, or he just doesn't like coming to school. What do you do?

Tip:

Set up a conference with the parent. Include other teachers or staff who can support your concerns through their experiences.

Gather all documentation. Be sure to check the office for the student's permanent file, where records are kept from year to year. Bring in the portfolio and check the student's folders from the previous year to see if there is a pattern. Also, look at the previous year's standardized test scores, if they are posted. Show your compassion for the child and the parent. You may want to use an analogy to help them understand the situation. Explain how learning throughout the school year can be compared to building a bridge. As your students learn, they are building their academic skills—the bridge—to the next grade level. They must progress at a certain rate so they'll complete their bridge by the end of the year and make a smooth transition to the next grade. Gently tell the parent that his child is not progressing at a rate that will carry him across that bridge and into the next grade. Assure the parent that you want only what is best for his child, and that the educational system has programs to assist every child at every level in reaching his full academic potential. You want him to receive the help that will support him in meeting all the goals and standards for this year.

Snapshot #46:

The Parent Wants Her Child to Skip a Grade

Follow the experts' guidelines.

A parent wants to meet with you, making it the third conference in three months, to once again discuss the same topic. She insists her child would be better off skipping a grade next year. She bases her argument on the fact that her child is a year ahead in her reading, the work she's doing in all areas is too easy, she is always the first student finished, and she does her homework in school. The parent contends that her child needs to be challenged and keeping her in her current grade level is not beneficial. You don't believe this is in the child's best interest and must explain your position to the parent. What do you do?

Tip :

At this third conference, explain that you are making the determination based on this year's performance and also on the years to come.

You agree she is functioning well in the advanced reading group and her math skills are progressing. Because academic skills are built upon those previously learned, when a child skips a grade, she may not be taught some of those skills. You can use learning long division as an example, showing how the student must be able to estimate and multiply. These skills may not be acquired if she skips a grade. Ask the parent if she has considered the social, emotional, and physical aspects of pushing her child ahead in school. While having her child as the youngest child in her class right now may not cause problems, she should project what it will be like for the child when she's in middle school and high school. Socially, she will be thrust into situations, such as having friends who can drive, date, and stay out late, or being offered liquor or drugs, a year before her peers face those difficult situations. Will she be emotionally mature enough to make the right choices? If she is inclined toward sports, she will always be competing against children who are older, bigger, and more experienced, making it tough for her to excel. By discussing these issues, the parent may have a change of heart. But if she does not, have the parent request a conference with the principal.

Notes:
_____

_____

_____

_____

_____

_____

_____

_____

_____

✱ Things to do for April:

CHAPTER NINE
May: Special Projects-For Student Use Only

> "The real art of conversation is not only to say the right thing at the right place but to leave unsaid the wrong thing at the tempting moment."
> Dorothy Nevill

Overview

This chapter deals with special and monthly group projects. We will explore the importance of explaining to parents how rubrics, group interaction, and cooperative teamwork are an integral building block of the learning experience. Most importantly, you will learn how to emphasize to the student and the parent that any schoolwork should be done by students only. You will be able to guide the parents in their role as a facilitator and not a doer. You will learn how to talk with parents when:

www.school-talk.com

The Snapshots:

47. A child is given another opportunity on a project.

48. A child plagiarizes work for her project.

49. A child representing the school at an academic competition doesn't adhere to the dress code.

50. A parent complains that her child did all the work on a group project yet has to share the grade.

51. A parent asks, "Why are oral presentations always required?"

52. A parent emails you using an inappropriate tone.

Snapshot #47:
A Child Is Given Another Opportunity on a Project

Mr. Hall shows up at your classroom, angrily accusing you of giving the wrong grade for his child's science fair project, stating he knows his son did the project as he, the parent, personally supervised it. He demands that you give the project an A. What should you do?

Tip :

If possible, do not address this problem with the parent in the hallway or at the door of the classroom.

Ask to set up a conference for a later date. If you are able to conduct the conference at that moment, give yourself ten minutes to get the documentation together. If documentation is not immediately available, schedule the conference for the next day. At the conference, show the rubric you devised, letting the parent know up front that you wanted a child's project, not the parent's. Clarify that the rough draft was done in school and reviewed. The assignment at home was to polish and complete it. Inform the parent that the project was done incorrectly and that the child can try again without being penalized. Emphasize that your goal is for the child to succeed no matter how long it takes. Remind the parent that children learn at different rates, and as long as the child becomes proficient in the skill, that is what counts.

www.school-talk.com

Snapshot #48:

A Child Plagiarizes Work for Her Project

Y ou assign your students a term paper giving a complete rubric describing exactly what it takes to receive an A, B, or C grade. One of the criteria states that the student must put the information into her own words, and you reinforce this information with a lesson in class, so all of the students understand its importance. You send home the rubric with each child and post it on your homework site. You also show an example of an A paper to the class so students know exactly what is expected. A child hands in a paper that clearly is not in her own words or writing style. You give her an F. The parent calls and wants to know why his child received an F, saying, "I thought it was a great paper. She worked very hard on it. The facts are there, as well as illustrations, and she handed it in on time. I just don't understand. You seem to be picking on my daughter." What do you do?

Tip : **Call the parent and the child in together.**

Show the parent the rubric and highlight the parts that his daughter did not follow, including the part concerning plagiarism. Ask the child to explain how she went about finding the information, organizing her thoughts, and constructing the term paper. Ask her if she understands what the term "plagiarism" means. After bringing up these points, show the parent his daughter's paper and the location of a website where you found the exact words on the topic his daughter wrote about. Explain that this is why you had to give the child an F, but that she can have another chance. Tell both parent and child your expectations and review the rubric. Use the **Rubric Grading Design Form** *(Worksheet #32)* as a guide. Impress upon both that completing this assignment will assist her with future term papers. Developing writing skills will help the student in all her classes, not just now, but when she gets to college. Remind them that if the revised paper is not turned in by the deadline, the F stands.

Snapshot #49:

A Child Representing the School at an Academic Competition Doesn't Adhere to the Dress Code

Tip:

Remain cool, but be firm. Remind Mercedes that a letter was sent home with her specifying the school's dress code for such events.

She cannot represent the school dressed as she is, even though she may be one of the top competitors. If time permits, allow her to call home and ask someone to bring her the proper attire. Stand by in case the parent wants further explanation. If no one responds to her call, or if there is no time for her to get a change of clothes, she must be sent home.

A t 8:30 a.m. Mercedes meets the group that will be representing the school at the math competition. She is dressed inappropriately, wearing jeans and a cutoff top. A letter had been sent home stipulating the proper dress for the competition. What do you do?

Save all written communication sent home.

Second chances are acceptable as long as the student learns an important principle.

115

Snapshot #50:

A Parent Complains That Her Child Did All the Work on a Group Project Yet Has to Share the Grade

Julie's mom is clearly upset when she shows up at your classroom and launches into her complaint. "Why does my child have to work in a group? She always gets partnered up with kids who don't do the work. She winds up doing the whole thing. What value is there for her in this kind of arrangement? It's just not fair to her; the other students use her talents and waste her time. I don't want her doing this anymore." What do you do?

Tip :

Tell the parent that because you want to discuss this in depth with her, you'd like to schedule a conference so you won't be interrupted and the meeting remains confidential.

In the conference, talk about the value of group projects for teaching students how to work with others, analyze the assignment, delegate tasks, conduct research, and design a project board. Group work also teaches children how to take on responsibility, to communicate effectively with others, and to think as a group, which often takes students beyond their normal scope. Such work will also help a student gain confidence when addressing, first, the other students in the group, and then the entire class, during the group presentation. In this case, point out that the group process has helped her child develop leadership skills that are critical for a successful future. If the parent is still unconvinced, suggest that the next time her child feels she's doing too much of the work, she should let you know. You will facilitate the group interaction and help the others become better organized and learn how to help each other. You can also help them by allowing them to go to the library and retrieve the materials they need or by distributing necessary art supplies. Stress that group work not only supports academic learning, but other lessons as well, such as how to develop discipline, build character, and acquire communication skills, all of which will serve the students throughout life.

Snapshot #51:

A Parent Asks, "Why Are Oral Presentations Always Required?"

Tip:

Tell the parent that it is especially important for his daughter to acquire this skill; otherwise, her fear will continually cripple her educational performance.

Jenny's father calls you to set up a conference to talk about his daughter's presentation skills. At the conference he says, "My daughter is extremely shy and hates to speak in front of a group. It doesn't seem fair to judge her on her oral presentation when this is such a difficult task for her. She has begged me to talk to you so she won't have to do this any longer. Surely you can exempt her from this and base her grade upon something else." What do you do?

Encouragement is a good thing.

By learning to speak in front of a group, she will build the self-confidence she clearly needs. Convince her father that you can help his daughter through the exercise in a number of ways: by giving her prompts, by making her presentation more like a dialogue with you, by asking her questions so she can give the answers without feeling pressured to memorize and deliver the whole presentation on her own. Share any experiences you may have had that support your case; perhaps you had a shy child like his daughter in a previous class who, through practice, could speak on her own in front of the class by the end of the year and was rewarded by her classmates applauding her effort. This is what you want for his child, and you can help by finding that initial comfort level for her.

Snapshot #52:

A Parent Emails You Using an Inappropriate Tone

Great communication takes effort.

You log onto your computer and find an email message from Xavier's mom, written in a very negative and accusatory tone: "Xavier hates coming to school. You pressure him too much in class. You constantly misunderstand his needs, which isn't surprising, as apparently you don't understand children in general. I say this because I spoke to many other parents of children in your class and they all feel the same way. I am sending a copy of this to the administration. I want a meeting with you as soon as possible." Angry and hurt, you reply by email, using the same tone: "I try to do my best and wonder why you haven't come to me with your concerns. I think you'll find that I consistently follow the class rules. Perhaps the problem stems from the fact that your child's grades are dropping. I wrote about this in several reports to you, but you have not responded. As to my qualifications as a teacher, many parents have told me I am one of the best teachers they've ever known. I would be more than happy to document these comments!"

Tip : **First, never put an emotional response in writing, especially on email, that can be downloaded and easily circulated by a parent.**

Anything you write must be defended, as it can become evidence. Second, wait to respond. Clearly the parent is reacting emotionally. But you are the professional educator; don't respond with the same anger and frustration the parent exhibited. Get a hard copy of the email for your files and future conferencing. Respond by thanking her for her interest and making a request to conference with her and an administrator as soon as possible to discuss the situation. Let your administrator know what occurred and ask for him to be at the meeting, if possible. If that's not possible, ask for advice on how to handle the conference.

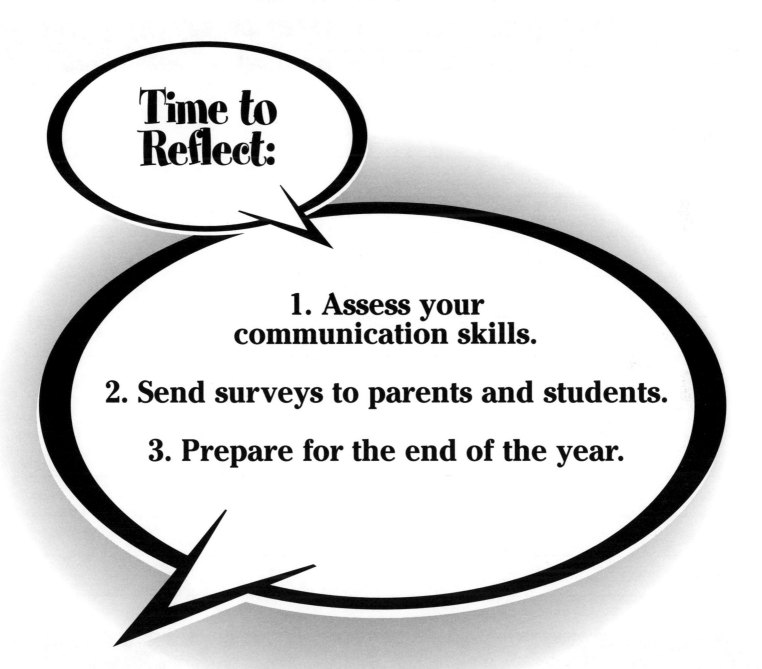

Time to Reflect:

1. Assess your communication skills.

2. Send surveys to parents and students.

3. Prepare for the end of the year.

Notes:

✳ Things to do for May:

CHAPTER TEN
June: Reflections–Communicate With Thyself

> "Among my most prized possessions are words that I have never spoken."
> Orson Rega Card

Overview

As you turn the calendar to the last month of school, you find yourself counting the days until summer vacation. You reflect on the year gone by, particularly on your conferences with parents and students. Did you feel that you developed the art of communicating effectively, or were there snapshots in which you still found yourself inadequate? This chapter will provide you with the tools for your personal growth in effective communication that will assist you with your continuing professional development.

www.school-talk.com

Your Tools Are:

- **The Parent Communication Survey**

- **The Student Communication Survey (Lower Grades)**

- **The Student Communication Survey (Upper Grades)**

- **The Quarterly Self-Evaluation Checklist**

- **The Communication Skills Assessment**

The **Parent Communication Survey** *(Worksheet #36)* and the **Student Communication Survey** *(Worksheets #37 and #38)* both function much like a customer satisfaction evaluation. They give your "customers" an opportunity to tell you what is working and what is not. In conducting the surveys, you will learn how to collect data and analyze it, develop a student tracking sheet, and interpret the results for your own personal growth.

The **Quarterly Self-Evaluation Checklist** *(Worksheet #2)* will assist you in tracking your own development. We recommend that you utilize this tool each quarter for self-analysis while you track your growth. You may also want to keep a daily journal and write about your communication experiences.

How do others see you? It takes courage to be willing to listen and make changes based on others' opinions of ourselves. If you are not ready to venture on this journey just yet, you may want to ask one of your most trusted friends for an honest opinion.

We would like to leave you with these final thoughts: Have you ever encountered a situation where you were talking to someone but not getting your point across, or you felt as though you were speaking in a foreign language, because your listener clearly did not understand what you were trying to say? Remember, you hold within yourself the key to effective communication. Only you have the power to communicate your thoughts and ideas to others—no one else can do this for you. The good news is that anyone who is willing to make some changes and has the determination to succeed can master this essential skill. You will find that when you change your communication techniques and style for the better, your listeners will react accordingly.

We want you to be effective in all your communications. By using the information we share in this book, you can approach any situation that requires good communication skills with confidence.

Notes: _____

_____

_____

_____

_____

_____

_____

_____

_____

_____

✻ Things to do for June:

☐ _____

☐ _____

☐ _____

☐ _____

☐ _____

☐ _____

☐ _____

☐ _____

☐ _____

☐ _____

☐ _____

☐ _____

☐ _____

☐ _____

☐ _____

☐ _____

☐ _____

☐ _____

☐ _____

☐ _____

☐ _____

☐ _____

☐ _____

☐ _____

Epilogue

www.school-talk.com

May you continue your journey of communicating effectively with everyone who crosses your path. The more you practice the tools and techniques provided here, the better communicator you will become. By communicating effectively, you will not only serve your own needs, but you will be better equipped to serve those of your students and their parents.

We send our best wishes for your continued growth from every communication opportunity that comes your way. We would love to hear from you! How did the book help you? What were your favorite snapshots? What tips or worksheets did you like best? Please send us your comments.

You can write to us at:

School Talk
9737 N.W. 41 Street, #356
Miami, FL 33178

We look forward to effectively communicating with You!

Share Your Snapshots

Your Snapshot

How do you make communication easier?

We invite you to share with us your snapshots. Please let us know what situations you have dealt with, what tools you have developed, and what worksheets you use to make your communications easier.

We would love to feature you in our next book. **Please send submissions to: School-Talk at submissions@school-talk.com**

Visit us at our **website: http://www.school–talk.com** and sign up for our **FREE** newsletter, *School Talk!*, or personally email Cheli and Ruth at:
Cheli at: *Cheli@School-Talk.com*
Ruth at: *Dr.Ruth@School-Talk.com*

We hope that you have enjoyed reading *Teacher Talk!* as much as we have enjoyed writing it.

APPENDIX A
Worksheets to Complete Your Files

Appendix A

Worksheets to Complete Your Files

Appendix A

Worksheets to Complete Your Files

WORSHEET #1:
Communication Skills Assessment Pre-Test/Post-Test

Directions: Check "Y" for Yes and "N" for No to give the answer you find most appropriate.

☐Y ☐N   1.   I am comfortable speaking with parents.

☐Y ☐N   2.   I listen more than I talk.

☐Y ☐N   3.   I value parent input.

☐Y ☐N   4.   I encourage parents to visit my classroom.

☐Y ☐N   5.   I anticipate and welcome questions.

☐Y ☐N   6.   I come prepared to meetings.

☐Y ☐N   7.   I research solutions and methods when I do not know the answers.

☐Y ☐N   8.   I like to invite parents to shows and have presentations/expos frequently.

☐Y ☐N   9.   I do not believe that I know more than parents do.

☐Y ☐N   10.   I do not mind if an administrator sits in on a parent conference.

☐Y ☐N   11.   I make eye contact during parent meetings.

☐Y ☐N   12.   I respect the opinions of parents.

☐Y ☐N   13.   I don't feel uncomfortable when people are in my classroom.

☐Y ☐N   14.   I smile and greet parents and students each morning and afternoon.

☐Y ☐N   15.   I initiate parent contact immediately, as concerns arise.

☐Y ☐N   16.   I am at ease when talking with parents about difficult situations.

☐Y ☐N   17.   I communicate frequently with parents.

☐Y ☐N   18.   I admit to parents that I do not know an answer and get back to them when I find out information they need.

☐Y ☐N   19.   I am comfortable talking with teachers/principals/specialists.

☐Y ☐N   20.   I like to invite parents into the classroom.

Count up the number of "Yes" answers, and then find the corresponding comments below.

If you scored 18 or higher, you are on your way to becoming an effective communicator.

If you scored 15 to 18, you may want to read carefully those chapters addressing areas in which you are weak and practice the authors' techniques. The other chapters may give you further insight and communication skills to benefit your own conversational style.

If you scored below 15, you will want to read all the chapters. Practice the techniques, asking your colleagues to assist you. When you're ready to use the techniques, you may want to start by applying them in more simple situations or by talking to those parents with whom you feel comfortable before you tackle the more difficult situations.

WORKSHEET #2:
Quarterly Self-Evaluation Checklist

Answer these questions at the end of each reporting quarter.

1. What instrumental techniques am I using?
   Most often:_____
   Not enough: _____
2. What works best? _____
3. What works least?_____
4. How can I improve?_____
5. Am I a change agent?_____
6. Am I consistent with communicating routines?_____
   Place a check for Yes. If not, have suggestions on how you can improve.
   ☐ Homework   ☐ Discipline
   ☐ Newsletters   ☐ Lessons
   ☐ Parents (conferences)   ☐ Emails
   ☐ Websites
7. Am I looking at the **Individual Tracking Sheet** and **Class Tracking Sheet** (*Worksheets #33 and #34*)
   to see if students are achieving seventy-five percent or higher on test scores?_____
   If not met, what strategies will I use to increase scores?_____
8. Am I incorporating parental assistance?_____
9. Am I grading and assessing in a timely fashion and communicating results to students
   and parents?_____
10. Am I setting high expectations for classroom performance? _____

WORKSHEET #3:
Countdown to the First Day of School Checklist

DAY 10: Have bulletin board paper and any prefabricated commercial products on hand.
☐ Set aside a file box for portfolios and blank folders.
TIP: *Don't put names on until the last minute.*

DAY 9: Plan the design for all the bulletin boards. Include a welcome sign and communication board on which you can put the newsletters, wish list, school flyers, and requests for volunteers. Place this board in a convenient area for parents; you will be letting them know that this is where they can find all recent communications sent home.
☐ Make a suggestion box for parent ideas.

DAY 8: Review the teacher's edition of all textbooks and workbooks.
☐ Create a Wish List sign, including pull-off tabs a parent can detach to fulfill the request. Example: a tree with apples, with each apple having a wish written on it (e.g., pencils, markers, Band-aids, towelettes, throw-away cameras). Some teachers have used keys, happy faces, or their classroom theme instead of the apple idea.

DAY 7: Prepare a homework in-box and out-box.

DAY 6: Write the first two weeks' curriculum plans.

DAY 5: Post your daily class schedule.
☐ Fill in the **Class List** *(Worksheet #4).*

DAY 4: Purchase folders and containers for in and out papers.

DAY 3: Familiarize yourself with school forms, the School Handbook, and the Code of Student Conduct.
☐ Formulate chart for class rules.
TIP: *The number of rules should be about the same as the age of the student. For example, if the children are five years old, there should be no more than five rules to follow. Make sure you state or write the rules in the positive. For example, instead of saying "No yelling," try "Quiet voices only."*

DAY 2: Prepare name tags, class roster, and grade book.
TIP: *Have extra name tags on hand for any additional students the office may assign to you. Design and type a welcome letter to parents. Ask a colleague to check the letter. She may have additional ideas and help you detect typing and spelling errors.*

DAY 1: Prepare Parent Packets. Parent Packet should include:
☐ **Letter of Introduction** *(Sample A)*
☐ **Classroom Rules/School Procedures**
☐ **Emergency Contact Form** *(Worksheet #6)*
☐ **Transportation Information Form** *(Worksheet #9)*
☐ **Volunteer Sign-Up Letter** *(Sample B)*

WORKSHEET #4:
Class List

Student Name	Parent Name(s)	Home Phone	Work/Cell Phone	Email	Birthday

ESL/LEP	Special Needs	Below Grade Level	Above Grade Level	On Grade Level	Conference Date(s)

WORKSHEET #5:
Open House Sign-In Form

Date: _____   Homeroom Teacher: _____   Grade: _____

Student Name	Parent Name	Parent Signature

WORKSHEET #6:
Emergency Contact Form

Student Name:_____

Parent Name(s): _____

Address: _____

Home Phone Number(s): _____

Email: _____

Emergency Contact: _____

Work:_____

Mother's Cell:_____

Father's Cell:_____

145

WORKSHEET #7:
Parent Request for Conference Form

Conference Sign-Up Form

Student name: _____

Parent name(s) *(please give full name)*: _____

Best time to meet:_____ **Best time to call:** _____

Best day of the week:_____

Parent concerns: _____

_____

_____

Thank you for taking the time to fill out this form for me.

Sincerely,

_____

WORKSHEET #8:
Teacher Request for Conference Form

Teacher name:_____

Email: _____

Phone number:_____ Best time to call:_____

My available conference times are: _____

_____

Teacher's reason for conference: _____

_____

_____

_____

_____

WORKSHEET #9:
Transportation Information Form

Student name:_____ Date: _____

Parent(s) name: _____

Signature: _____

Check one:

☐ Bus   ☐ Walk   ☐ Bike (with helmet)   ☐ Car   ☐ Car pool

Bus name/number: _____

If child walks to school, give route: _____

_____

List walking buddies or siblings and grade level:_____

_____

If child bikes to school, give route (helmet must be worn): _____

_____

List bike buddies or siblings and grade level: _____

Car pool—give parent name(s): _____

_____

_____

Parents, if the information changes, please let _____ know immediately.

(Teacher's Name)

WORKSHEET #10:
Communication to Parents for Setting a Conference

Date: _____ To the parents of: _____

From: _____

Student name: _____

Teacher name: _____ Grade: _____

I would like to meet with you to discuss the following concerns:

1. _____

2. _____

3. _____

Here are the days and times I can meet with you:

1. _____

2. _____

3. _____

Daytime phone: _____

Evening phone: _____

Email: _____

Looking forward to hearing from you soon.

Sincerely,

Teacher's Signature: _____

WORKSHEET #11:
Parent/Teacher Phone Log

Student Name	Parent Name	Date/Time	Spoke to	Outcome

WORKSHEET #12:
Classroom Newsletter

What We Learned This Week In:

Math: _____

Reading: _____

Science: _____

Writing: _____

Social Studies: _____

Computers: _____

Outstanding Student Achievements:

Upcoming Class Events:

Upcoming School Events:

Important Things to Remember:

Student of the Week:

Volunteers Needed For:

WORKSHEET #13:
Volunteer Guidelines Sheet

Thank you for expressing an interest in volunteering in our classroom. Parent involvement adds a lot to the student's academic experience, and we look forward to working with you to make this school year one of your child's best.

The following are a few guidelines to help you know what you can expect and what is expected of you. We have found that following these simple rules makes the volunteering process more enjoyable for everyone.

- **Please refrain from talking about the children to other parents. This is a common courtesy all of us would want extended to our own children.**

- **Follow the teacher's instructions.**

- **Ask for advice if you run into a situation that needs clarification.**

- **If you would like to do something special, ask the teacher so you can plan the event together.**

- **Don't handle a student's misbehavior. Instead, inform the teacher immediately.**

- **Always let the teacher know when you are coming into the classroom.**

- **If you are expected, always let the teacher know if you will be absent. The teacher depends on you, as do the children.**

WORKSHEET #14:
Volunteer Thank-You Gram

Date: _____

Dear Volunteer:_____

Thank You—You Made a Difference!

Thank you so much for assisting me. You certainly made a difference in my day

and in the lives of my students. We look forward to having you come back soon.

Sincerely,

_____

(Teacher's Name)

WORKSHEET #15:
Day of the Conference Checklist

Are you ready? Use the following checklist to prepare for a conference.

☐ **YES** ☐ **NO**   **1.** Prepare by using the **Conference Action Plan** *(Worksheet #19)*.

☐ **YES** ☐ **NO**   **2.** Prepare a portfolio with sample work and assessments of the student. Use the **Portfolio Checklist** to assist you *(Worksheet #31)*.

☐ **YES** ☐ **NO**   **3.** Prepare a space that is quiet and where there will be no disruptions.
Put up a sign: Conference Taking Place: Do Not Disturb.
Inform the school secretary so you can be contacted, if needed.

☐ **YES** ☐ **NO**   **4.** Arrange the chairs in a circle. You do not want to sit behind a desk.

☐ **YES** ☐ **NO**   **5.** Establish a start time and end time.

☐ **YES** ☐ **NO**   **6.** Make sure parent names are correct.

☐ **YES** ☐ **NO**   **7.** Be prepared to listen, listen, listen.

☐ **YES** ☐ **NO**   **8.** State your concern without calling it a problem. You don't want to diagnose.

☐ **YES** ☐ **NO**   **9.** Provide recommendations.

☐ **YES** ☐ **NO**   **10.** Schedule a follow-up meeting to assess progress in student.

TIP: *Thank parents for cooperating and attending the meeting. Remember to shake their hands.*

WORKSHEET #16:
Discipline Referral Form

Student name: _____ Date:_____

Teacher name:_____ Grade: _____

Description of incident: _____

_____

_____

_____

Action taken by teacher: _____

_____

_____

_____

Is this a repeat offense?	☐ Yes	☐ No
Has student had other behavior problems?	☐ Yes	☐ No
Has parent been contacted before for misbehavior?	☐ Yes	☐ No

If yes, when?_____.

Result of that contact:_____

_____

_____

_____

Administrative disciplinary action: _____

_____

_____

_____

Signature: _____

Time sent out of class: _____ Time sent back to class: _____

155

WORKSHEET #17:
Incident Communication Report

Student name: _____ Date: _____

Teacher name: _____ Grade: _____

Description of incident: _____

_____

_____

_____

How it was handled in school: _____

_____

_____

_____

Suggestions for parents: _____

_____

_____

_____

Parent contacted: ☐ Yes   ☐ No

Spoke with: _____
                                        (Name)

Date: _____ Time: _____ How: _____

Teacher's signature: _____ Date: _____

Parent's signature: _____ Date: _____

Administrator's signature: _____ Date: _____

WORSHEET #18:
Conference Reminder Form

We have scheduled the following time to discuss _____.

(*Student*)

Date: _____ Time: _____

Place: _____

I look forward to meeting with you.

Sincerely,

_____

(*Teacher's Signature*)

WORKSHEET #19:
Conference Action Plan

Child's name: _____

Grade: _____

Teacher's name: _____

Date: _____

Purpose: _____

_____

Goals: _____

_____

Observation: _____

_____

Type of conference (Check one):

☐ Mandatory   ☐ Behavior

☐ Academic   ☐ Medical

☐ Other _____

☐ **Portfolio available:** *Dated with current samples of work*

Fill in academic grades for:

Reading _____

Quizzes _____

Writing _____

H.W. samples _____

Math _____

Projects _____

Tests _____

Rubrics _____

Student is doing well in: _____

Student needs work on: _____

Action Plan:

For Home:

1. _____

2. _____

3. _____

For School:

1. _____

2. _____

3. _____

Suggestions:

1. _____

2. _____

3. _____

Date for the follow-up phone conference:

_____

Parent's signature: _____

Date: _____

Teacher's signature: _____

Date: _____

WORKSHEET #20:
Behavior Observation Chart

Student's name: _____ Grade: _____ Date: _____

TIME	MONDAY	TUESDAY	WEDNESDAY	THURSDAY	FRIDAY	BEHAVIOR
8:00 am 8:30 am						
8:30 am 9:00 am						
9:00 am 9:30 am						
9:30 am 10:00 am						
10:00 am 10:30 am						
10:30 am 11:00 am						
11:00 am 11:30 am						
11:30 am 12:00 pm						
12:00 pm 12:30 pm						
12:30 pm 1:00 pm						
1:00 pm 1:30 pm						
1:30 pm 2:00 pm						
2:00 pm 2:30 pm						
2:30 pm 3:00 pm						

Parent's Signature: _____ Teacher's Signature: _____

WORKSHEET #21:
Behavior Contract

Date: _____

I, _____ , promise to _____
       (Student)
_____
_____
_____

If the student follows the contract, the following rewards will take place:

1. _____
2. _____
3. _____

If the student does not follow the contract, the following consequences will take place:

1. _____
2. _____
3. _____

Date to see changes and review: _____

Follow-up date to revise contract: _____

_____   _____
Student's Signature   *Teacher's Signature*

_____   _____
Parent's Signature   *Administrator's/Designee's Signature*

WORKSHEET #22:
Academic Communication Checklist

Student's name: ——————————————————————————————

Teacher's name: ——————————————————————————————

Week of: ——————————————————————————————————

SUBJECT	EXCELLENT	AVERAGE	FAILING	COMMENTS
English				
Math				
Reading				
Science				
Social Studies				
Writing				
Other				

Parent's Signature: ———————————————————— Date: ————————

161

WORKSHEET #23:
Student Behavioral Insight Form

Student's name:_____ **Grade:**_____ **Date:**_____

Teacher's name:_____

My incorrect behavior was: _____

I did not follow the following classroom rule:_____

Because of my behavior, I now feel:_____

Another classmate feels:_____

The teacher feels:_____

My parents will feel:_____

Next time I will:_____

Student's signature: _____

Teacher's signature: _____

Parent's signature: _____

Person contacted about incident: _____

Date:_____**Time:**_____   *(Name)*

Method of communication: ☐ **Email**   ☐ **Phone**   ☐ **Voice mail** ☐ **Other:**_____

162

WORKSHEET #24:
Reminder for a Misbehavior Form

Class rule broken is: _____

Every time I break this class rule, I will:

1. _____

2. _____

3. _____

Student's signature: _____ **Date:** _____

Teacher's signature: _____ **Date:** _____

Parent's signature: _____ **Date:** _____

WORKSHEET #25:
Work Habits Anecdotal Checklist (Elementary)

Student's Name: _____ Grade: _____ Date: _____

TIME	List Work Habits	On Task	Needs Improvement	Comments
8:00 am 8:30 am				
8:30 am 9:00 am				
9:00 am 9:30 am				
9:30 am 10:00 am				
10:00 am 10:30 am				
10:30 am 11:00 am				
11:00 am 11:30 am				
11:30 am 12:00 pm				
12:00 pm 12:30 pm				
12:30 pm 1:00 pm				
1:00 pm 1:30 pm				
1:30 pm 2:00 pm				
2:00 pm 2:30 pm				
2:30 pm 3:00 pm				

Parent's Signature:_____ Teacher's Signature: _____

WORKSHEET #26:
Work Habits Anecdotal Checklist (Middle/High)

Student's Name: _____ Grade:_____ Date: _____

SUBJECT	List Work Habits	On Task	Needs Improvement	Comments
Reading				
Math				
Social Studies				
Science				
Lunch				
Elective				
Elective				
Elective				
Elective				

Parent's Signature: _____

Teacher's Signature: _____

165

WORKSHEET #27:
Preliminary Anecdotal Record

Student:_____ **Date:**_____

Observer: _____

_____

Area of concern: _____

_____

Date: _____ **Time:** _____

Date: _____ **Time:** _____

Date: _____ **Time:** _____

WORKSHEET #28:
Behavior Observation/Anecdotal Record

Student Name: _____

Observed by: _____

TIME	DATE	BEHAVIOR

WORKSHEET #29:
Student School Readiness Task Chart

Routine for the Night Before:

☐ Did I finish my homework?

☐ Did my mom/dad initial my homework?

☐ Did I give my mom/dad all the papers and flyers the teacher gave out today?

☐ Do I have my lunch money?

☐ Did I put my clothes out for tomorrow?

☐ Is my backpack ready and placed by the front door?

☐ Does the backpack have:

    ☐ Homework?

    ☐ Pencils?

    ☐ Folders?

    ☐ Textbooks?

    ☐ A book from home?

☐ Did I set my alarm clock?

Morning Routine:

☐ Did I brush my teeth?

☐ Did I brush my hair?

☐ Did I eat breakfast?

☐ Did I clear the table?

When I have completed all of the tasks, I can: _____

_____

_____

_____

_____

_____

_____

_____

_____

WORKSHEET #30:
Missed Homework Alert Form

Student's Name: _____ **Date:** _____

Teacher's Name: _____

Homework Missed: _____

_____

_____

_____

_____

_____

Your child has missed two (2) homework assignments. Please check to see that assignments are completed on time and represent your child's best work.

If you would like to schedule a conference, please call me at [phone #] or send a note to school.

Respectfully,

_____
(Teacher's Signature)

WORKSHEET #31:
Portfolio Checklist

- [ ] 1. Copies of all communications to parents from teacher

- [ ] 2. Copies of all communications to teacher from parent

- [ ] 3. Tracking sheets

- [ ] 4. Sample of reading, writing, math, (one of each per quarter)
    a. Four samples of best work
    b. Five samples of work that shows growth

- [ ] 5. Rubrics for assignment

- [ ] 6. Major projects with rubrics

- [ ] 7. Chapter tests

- [ ] 8. Assessments, evaluations, checklists, and rubrics

- [ ] 9. Date on all papers

- [ ] 10. Anecdotal records

- [ ] 11. Copies of parent-teacher conferences: report cards, interim reports

- [ ] 12. Copies of accident reports

TIP: *All sample work and communications must be dated.*

WORKSHEET #32:
Rubric Grading Design Form

The following project is due:

Description:_____

Theme:_____

Objective:_____

Learning Expectations:_____

State Standard:_____

The following letter grades will be awarded to work completed on time and meeting the specified criteria:

☐ **A** Meets all of the prerequisites for B and C grades, plus is correct in grammar and spelling with an easy flow of words and topics

☐ Extra research information given in oral presentation, supported with graphics

☐ Presentation was made in clear voice

☐ Presentation contained important information

☐ **B** Meets prerequisites for C grade, with inclusion of charts, pictures, subtitles, and memorized oral presentation

☐ All additional charts, etc., are clearly labeled

☐ **C** Meets minimum requirements for C grade

☐ Includes introduction and table of contents

☐ Written in child's own words, neatly organized, read in an oral presentation

☐ Meets minimum requirements for bibliography, number of pages, subheading

☐ **D or F** Opportunity to resubmit
Next due date is _____.
If you need assistance, see me before or after class and I will show you an A/B paper so you can compare yours.

171

WORKSHEET #33:
Individual Tracking Sheet

Student Name: _____

Directions: Using the school records, fill in the student's standardized test scores. This is a recommended resource that you may want to keep in order to track the student's history on previous standardized tests. A history can provide a wealth of information for conferences, determining skills level, and seeking knowledge on a child's performance record. This is an easy snapshot of a child's test history.

	Math Level	Reading Level	Writing Level	ESL/LEP Level	IEP Status	Other	Teacher
K							
1st							
2nd							
3rd							
4th							
5th							
6th							

WORKSHEET #34:
Class Tracking Sheet

Standardized Testing Percentiles

TEACHER:　　　　　　　　　　　**GRADE(S):**　　　**SCHOOL YEAR:**

	Student Name (Last, First)	ESL	LEP	IEP	Reading Level	Math Level	Writing Level
1							
2							
3							
4							
5							
6							
7							
8							
9							
10							
11							
12							
13							
14							
15							
16							
17							
18							
19							
20							
21							
22							
23							
24							
25							
26							
27							
28							

Note: Highlight in yellow any students who are below grade level. Write ESL/ LEP level or, if child has an IEP, state exceptionality/related services in the appropriate column.

173

WORKSHEET #35:
Standardized Test Explanations Form

How to explain to a parent what all those numbers mean:

National Percentile Rank (NPR)

This score demonstrates how your child did in comparison with children across the nation. The number indicates the percentage of students who received a score equivalent to or lower than your child's.

Stanine

Stanine stands for a standard of nine. It comes from the range of a low score of 1 to a high score of 9. A score that falls into the low category indicates a situation that needs attention. A conference with the parent is recommended. Example:

Scores of: 1 - 2 - 3 are LOW   4 - 5 - 6 are AVERAGE   7 - 8 - 9 are HIGH

Raw Score

This score reveals the exact number of points gained on the test questions for correct responses. It also divides up the total possible score into the content area tested. Each area receives a score for correct responses only.

Norm-Referenced Test

This shows one group of students' achievement on the test as compared to a national system.

WORKSHEET #36:
Parent Communication Survey

Directions: For each statement circle a rating.

1: Most Effective   **2: Effective**   **3: Needs Improvement**

3 2 1   Teacher was familiar with the philosophy of the school.

3 2 1   Teacher listed classroom rules.

3 2 1   Teacher communicated weekly with a newsletter about curriculum updates, upcoming events, helpful hints.

3 2 1   Teacher gave tips on how to volunteer.

3 2 1   Parents were welcomed visitors.

3 2 1   Teacher communicated about a change in child's academic progress and/or social behavior as soon as it became evident.

3 2 1   Projects were relevant.

3 2 1   Rubrics were provided.

3 2 1   Teacher allowed time to gain skills.

3 2 1   Teacher offered advice, as needed.

3 2 1   Teacher provided information at conferences on all assessments and had a variety of work in a portfolio.

3 2 1   Teacher communicated effectively to parents in all three categories:
  (a) written notes
  (b) planners
  (c) conferences

3 2 1   Teacher communicated to parents specific ideas for promoting their child's academic/behavioral development at home.

What was most successful in the classroom? _____
_____
_____

What would you like to see added? _____
_____
_____
_____

Comments: _____
_____
_____
_____
_____

175

WORSHEET #37:
Student Communication Survey – Lower Grades

Read the statements aloud and have the children circle the face that best answers how they feel. Tell them this will help you with the students you will teach next year.

Circle a happy face for "Yes" and the sad face for "No."

☺ "Yes"   ☹ "No"

☺☹ **Did the teacher remind you to copy the homework?**

☺☹ **Did the teacher talk to your mom and dad when they came to your classroom?**

☺☹ **Did the teacher send notes home about your class?**

☺☹ **Did your mom or dad sometimes have to sign your class work?**

☺☹ **Did the teacher say "Good morning" every day?**

☺☹ **Did the teacher smile and tell funny stories?**

What I like best about my teacher and school: _____

_____

What I did not like about my teacher and school: _____

_____

WORKSHEET #38:
Student Communication Survey – Upper Grades

Directions: For each statement circle a rating.

1: Most Effective   **2: Effective**   **3: Needs Improvement**

3 2 1   1. The teacher put the classroom rules on the board and followed them.

3 2 1   2. The teacher gave us homework every night and made sure we wrote it down in the homework journal/planner.

3 2 1   3. The teacher collected and marked the homework.

3 2 1   4. The teacher gave us rubrics so we knew exactly what items needed to go into a report or assignment.

3 2 1   5. The teacher wrote or called my parent(s) when I didn't follow the rules.

3 2 1   6. The teacher wrote or called my parent(s) when my grades went down or I failed an exam.

3 2 1   7. The teacher complimented me when I tried my best.

3 2 1   8. The teacher rewarded the class when we had good days.

3 2 1   9. The teacher kept the homework website up to date in case I needed help when I got home.

3 2 1   10. The teacher gave us newsletters and notes to take home every week.

WORKSHEET #39:
Successful Teacher Checklist

Am I:

☐ 1. Open to change and able to adapt to new ideas?

☐ 2. Continuing to promote change as the year progresses? Do I take the attitude "Nothing is set in stone?"

☐ 3. Meeting the needs of parents?

☐ 4. Meeting the needs of students?

☐ 5. Meeting the needs of administration?

☐ 6. Attending seminars for teaching growth?

☐ 7. Involving parents?

☐ 8. Reporting continually to parents about upcoming news, events, and student development?

☐ 9. Sending home newsletters regularly?

☐ 10. Signing planners?

☐ 11. Evaluating continually my own progress, allowing for constructive criticism, and incorporating changes into my teaching style and communication techniques?

☐ 12. Providing data with knowledge and confidence?

☐ 13. Providing conflict resolution?

☐ 14. Being accessible to parents and students?

☐ 15. Providing a monthly calendar of events to parents?

☐ 16. Providing monthly rubrics to parents?

☐ 17. Communicating successfully with parents the specific goals of their child, showing portfolios as a backup variable tool?

☐ 18. Presenting outstanding student work samples in the classroom?

☐ 19. Using a variety of assessment tools?

☐ 20. Using a variety of techniques in lesson delivery?

☐ 21. Conferencing and explaining to parents their child's progress without using the comparison of other children in the class?

☐ 22. Sharing ideas and knowledge with parents?

☐ 23. Willing to listen?

APPENDIX B
Communication Samples From Cheli's and Ruth's File Cabinets

Appendix B

Communication Samples from Cheli's and Ruth's File Cabinets

Sample A

Letter of Introduction

To the Parents of Jim Garcia:

Welcome back to a new school year. My name is Mrs. Yvona Teach and I will be your child's first grade teacher this year. I have been teaching first grade at Sunnyside Elementary School for six years. Some of you may remember me from last year. I am very excited to start this new year and am confident that it will be a fun and productive one for your child.

I am looking forward to teaching your child how to read, do math problems, conduct science experiments, and do social studies projects. Many of the skills your child will learn this year will come from our new reading program. Over the summer, I attended a week-long workshop to learn many new teaching techniques. I can't wait to share them with you at our Open House that has been scheduled for October 11th. Details about the Open House and other exciting happenings will be in our weekly class newsletter. Look for it every Friday in your child's backpack.

It is my goal to make our classroom a positive learning environment. Please feel free to contact me before or after school if you have any questions or concerns.

I look forward to meeting you at Open House on October 11th.

Sincerely,

Mrs. Yvona Teach

Sample B

Volunteer Sign-Up Letter

To the Parents of _____

(Child's Name)

We are looking for some very special people to help us in our classroom. Do you have some extra time, a special talent, or an eagerness to make a difference in the life of a child? We gladly welcome volunteers. Your time and effort would be greatly appreciated. If you can help us in any of the areas listed below, please indicate your choice and interests and return this form to your child's homeroom teacher. Please consider participating in some way. Our children need your help!

Sincerely, _____

(Tear Off)

- -

Name:_____ **Child's Name:** _____

Work Number: _____ **Home Number:**_____

☐ **Yes, I would like to gladly volunteer. I am available to**
  (please put a check next to each area that you are interested in)

☐ **Read to a Child:** **Day** _____ ☐ **Weekly Volunteer Available:** **Day**_____
              Time _____   **Time**_____

☐ **Help with Clubs** ☐ **Volunteer to be a Room Parent**

☐ **Chaperone a Field Trip** ☐ **Other:** _____

Suggestions: _____

_____

_____

Sample C

Guidelines for Medication Letter

Date: _____ **To the Parents of:** _____

Dear Parent(s):

We would like to inform you of the specific guidelines for administering medication at our school. These guidelines have come from the school district and are written below:

Don't send your child to school with medication without reading the important information that follows.

The Board of Education does not permit any unauthorized personnel to administer medication in any form to a student, not even an aspirin. There needs to be on record a medical authorization form signed by a doctor and dated.

The medicine must be brought to school in the original prescription bottle with a label that includes the name of the doctor, date, pharmacy name and number, and the correct instructions. The child's full name must appear as well. Transferring medication into a smaller container is not allowed.

Authorized school staff will keep the medicine locked up or refrigerated in a safe place. They will be the only ones who will dispense all medications and log them in the record book.

If you have any questions, please call the school's office. We are here to work together in the best interest of your child.

Sincerely,

_____

(Teacher)

Sample D

Behavior Occurrence Account Checklist

Student's Name: _____ **Grade:** _____ **Date:** _____

	Not Focused	Out of Seat	Calling Out	Bothering Others	Talking	Other
8:00 a.m. 8:30 am						
8:30 a.m. 9:00 a.m.						
9:00 a.m. 9:30 a.m.						
9:30 a.m. 10:00 a.m.						
10:00 a.m. 10:30 a.m.						
10:30 a.m. 11:00 a.m.						
11:00 a.m. 11:30 a.m.						
11:30 a.m. 12:00 p.m.						
12:00 p.m. 12:30 p.m.						
12:30 p.m. 1:00 p.m.						
1:00 p.m. 1:30 p.m.						
1:30 p.m. 2:00 p.m.						
2:00 p.m. 2:30 p.m.						
2:30 p.m. 3:00 p.m.						

Parent's Signature: _____ **Teacher's Signature:** _____

Sample E

Behavior Record Checklist

Directions: Put an (x) in the box on the days the behavior occurred.

Weekly Behavior Chart for: _____ **Date:** _____

	Monday	Tuesday	Wednesday	Thursday	Friday
Biting					
Hitting					
Out of Seat					
Yelling					
Incomplete Classwork					
Bothering Others					
Disrespectful to Teacher					
Using Profane Language					
(Other)					
(Other)					
(Other)					
(Other)					
(Other)					

Parent's Signature: _____

Teacher's Signature: _____

185

Sample F

Open House Checklist

In preparation for the Open House, make sure that you have available to discuss with parents the following:

- ☐ Students' work folders.
- ☐ Classroom rules posted for review. Be ready to discuss expectations for student behavior, rules, and homework requirements.
- ☐ Up-to-date bulletin boards.
- ☐ Curriculum books displayed in the front of the room for parents to view.

Share the following with parents:

1. Provide suitable space for your child's homework assignments. Refer to the **Improving Study Habits Checklist** *(Sample G)* as a guide.

2. Encourage reading at home. Read nightly to and with your child.

3. Establish a regular bedtime and stick to it. (e.g., 8:30 p.m. on school nights).

4. Give children a nutritious breakfast. Breakfast is a very important meal.

5. Regular attendance and punctuality are a must!

Do not discuss individual student problems! Set up a conference. Have available the **Parent Request for Conference Form** *(Worksheet #7).*

Encourage parent involvement in school and at home by sharing the **Volunteer Sign-Up Letter** *(Sample B).*

Please remind the parents of the Open House through letters, emails, and/or phone calls. It is an important meeting for them to attend. You want parents to be partners with you in their children's education.

Be positive.
Be encouraging and be sure to SMILE.
Have a great evening.

Sample G

Improving Study Habits Checklist

Directions: Put a check mark on each line before you begin studying.

I am ready to study when I have:

- ☐ A quiet area;
- ☐ A table or desk all to myself;
- ☐ Good lighting;
- ☐ Two sharpened pencils or a pen;
- ☐ Paper, notebooks, and folders;
- ☐ Schoolbooks needed for the assignment;
- ☐ Homework planner opened to today's date;
- ☐ Dictionary;
- ☐ Drink and snack on the table or desk;
- ☐ Timer; and
- ☐ Other supplies needed for any assignment (crayons, glue).

I will do my homework every night at _____ p.m.

I will review my class notes, study, or finish my homework by _____ .

Time

Sample H

Parent-Teacher Conference Form

Student's Name:_____ **Date:** _____
Teacher's Name:_____ **Grade:** _____

Directions: Place an N if student needs work on the skills below:

Work Habits
- [ ] listens
- [ ] is a self-starter
- [ ] does his/her best work
- [ ] uses time wisely
- [ ] works to his/her skill level
- [ ] other

Citizenship
- [ ] gets along well with classmates
- [ ] gets along well with teachers
- [ ] shows respect for self and others
- [ ] learns from mistakes
- [ ] accepts responsibility for own behavior
- [ ] other

Directions: Next to each subject, explain the skill level and write comments if necessary.

Reading_____ **Science**_____
Math _____ **Social Studies**_____
Writing _____ **Special Area**_____

Goals/Suggestions: _____
Parent's Signature:_____ **Date:**_____
Teacher's Signature:_____ **Date:**_____

Sample 1

Weekly Behavior Report

Student's Name: _____

Week of: _____

Monday:
Sally had a great day. Did all of her work; stayed focused and was well behaved.

Tuesday:
Sally did not complete her writing assignment; had difficulty staying focused; played with her pencil and scribbled her notes. When everyone else was working independently, she sat on the floor playing with her papers. The lunch staff reported she did not stay in her seat and hit someone. Overall, she had a difficult day.

Wednesday:
Sally had a good morning. Stayed in her seat; played well with her friends at recess. After lunch, she could not complete her work or follow directions; ran around the room and would not sit down. She had to be removed from class.

Thursday:
Sally came late to school. She had a difficult time joining the class in their daily routines.

Friday:
Sally forgot her math book and planner at home. She had a fairly good day and finished most of her work.

_____
Teacher's Signature

_____
Parent's Signature

Sample J

Conference Follow-Up Letter

Dear Parent(s) of: Donna Lee

I am very happy to share this news with you. In reviewing the last three test papers, it seems Donna has had a significant increase in her scores. Her attitude towards schoolwork has certainly changed. This change has occurred due to your efforts and continued assistance.

If this trend continues, I know we will all see an overall improvement on her report card.

Again, thank you for helping.

Sincerely,
Ms. Teach

Sample K

Letter of Congratulations

To the Parent(s) of: Bob Best

Congratulations! I have just received this year's test results, and I am thrilled to report to you that Bob scored in the top three percent of the country on the math standardized test. He achieved a high score of 97th percentile.

I am very proud of his achievement, as I am sure you are too. Together, as a team, we have made a difference. I know that this will be the first of many such terrific achievements for Bob.

Again, congratulations. I am very proud of him.

Sincerely,
Ms. Teach

Sample L

Response to Parent Letter

Dear Mr. Cartwright:

I have received your letter dated March 12th where you listed the concerns you had about your child and requested information on:

- ☐ **Homework policy**
- ☐ **Class discipline form**
- ☐ **Interim progress report**
- ☐ **Test scores**
- ☐ **Report cards**
- ☐ **Before-school programs**
- ☐ **Lunch program**
- ☐ **After-school programs**
- ☐ **Tardy report**
- ☐ **Transportation information**

I would like to review your concerns with you as soon as possible. Please call me at [phone #] in order for us to schedule a time to meet. I encourage parental involvement and look forward to working as a team.

Yours truly,
Mrs. Document

Sample M

Retention Warning Letter

Dear Mr. and Mrs. Kramer:

Each year at this time, we take a close look at the records of those pupils who may not be promoted at the end of the school year. A check of your child's marks indicates that she is not meeting our standards for promotion in June.

When talking to her teacher(s), the following items were mentioned as possible reasons for her failure:

☐ **poor test results**   ☐ **not working on grade level**
☐ **lack of participation**   ☐ **wasted time**
☐ **poor attendance**   ☐ **disturbing behavior**
☐ **not showing progress**   ☐ **other** _____

Because of your assistance in the past, we are asking you now to help to improve your child's skills. This notice is being sent to you today so that enough time remains for your child to improve in time to be promoted to the next grade.

Please call for a conference by calling [phone #].

I am looking forward to working with you.

Sincerely,
Ms. Teach

Sample N

Tardy Letter

Dear Mr. and Mrs. Son's-Tardy:

Today was _____ 's (   ) tardy to school.
(student's name)   *(number of tardies)*

Repeated lateness can hurt a child's academic performance and is

disruptive to the learning environment.

He has been previously tardy on: _____

_____

I am very concerned and would like to meet with you to discuss this

problem and, hopefully, arrive at a satisfactory solution. Please call me for

an appointment at [phone #].

Sincerely,

Ms. Teach

194

APPENDIX C
Bringing the Art of Communication to You

Programs Offered by Cheli and Ruth:

- Let's Talk!: Learning the Art of Effective Communication
- Teacher Talk!: Artfully Communicating with Parents
- Communication Blueprint for Success!

Here's what we want you to know more than anything else . . .

Dear Professional Development Coordinator:

Thank you for considering one of our breakthrough programs for your next event. We look forward to having the opportunity to offer your staff a motivational, thought-provoking, fun program rich in both content and humor. Our list of clients includes teachers, principals, superintendents, and others who want to become effective communicators.

We understand firsthand the freedom that comes with communicating effectively. Like you, we have been there in the trenches, and from our experiences, we have created a continuum of effective techniques thousands of individuals have used to achieve successful communication. But good communication is an ongoing exercise, and for people to continue to learn and to use the tools we offer, those tools must be easy to access. To that end, we have written the book *Teacher Talk!: The Art of Effective Communication*, which we can also have available to complement our program.

Learning how to effectively communicate is a necessity for the professional educator. People who know how to communicate well can head off problems before they arise, build strong relationships, create partnerships, and chart a path for students, parents, and teachers to travel together.

Which is a better expenditure of time, money, and effort: constantly having to remedy the problems that result from communication breakdowns, or being able to address difficult situations proactively through skilled communication? The choice is clear: knowing how to communicate effectively is essential, and we can teach your staff that skill.

Our programs have been tried and tested to provide you with first-class professional information and materials. You can choose from a wide variety of our proven courses or have us customize one for your staff's needs.

Contact us and tell us your communication challenge. We want to help you make your next professional development event a communication success!

Regards,
Cheli Cerra, M.Ed.
Ruth Jacoby, Ed.D.

P.S. When you want your people to communicate effectively, so that misunderstandings no longer steal time and create hard feelings, contact Cheli and Ruth for a customized, personalized, hands-on, humor-based keynote or seminar at their website, **http://www.school-talk.com.** The quicker you respond, the faster your staff will begin to learn how to communicate effectively.

Our Programs Are First-Class

Let's Talk!: Learning the Art of Effective Communication.

A successful communicator knows his audience and how to get his point across without creating any misunderstandings. In this hands-on, fun, and informative program, your staff will learn the tools necessary to begin artfully communicating with others. They will learn how to:

- **Use key words to defuse hostile situations;**
- **Listen effectively;**
- **Clearly convey their point to get their message heard; and**
- **Create positive relationships through effective communication.**

Cheli and Ruth use hands-on, personal experiences and real-life case studies to demonstrate and teach the tools necessary in learning the art of effective communication.

Book this program for your next meeting or convention and let Cheli and Ruth teach the staff within your organization the steps necessary to diffuse hostile situations, learn the art of listening, and create a positive communication-friendly environment.

www.school-talk.com

Teacher Talk!: Artfully Communicating with Parents.

This insightful program is designed to impact teachers at all levels. It assists the new teacher with effective communication tools and rejuvenates the veteran teacher by providing tools, techniques, and strategies that work.

The power of this program comes from real-life in-the-trenches solutions to common and uncommon communication problems. In this practical hands-on program, your teachers will leave with a practical action plan to begin effectively communicating with parents. The participants will learn communication tools that will make them:

• **Proactive;**
• **Organized;**
• **A good record-keeper; and**
• **An accurate reporter of information.**

Cheli and Ruth will provide assessments, tools, and practical techniques that help participants to organize their thoughts and follow a point-by-point plan for communicating effectively. Like thousands of others who have gone through the program, you will master a proven system to achieve the art of effective communication and establish a positive working relationship with parents.

Communication Blueprint for Success!

In this eye-opening workshop, the presenters will provide the participants with a self-assessment skills test that will reveal their personal communication comfort level. From this self-assessment, the audience will begin to map their own personal blueprint for communication success.

Cheli and Ruth use situations, snapshots, and activities to involve the audience. This interactive workshop is fun and informative. Participants will learn how to:

• **Use key phrases to capture attention;**
• **Talk effortlessly through difficult communication situations; and**
• **Learn the number-one secret to effective communication.**

Book this program for your staff today and have them leave with a personal communication blueprint that they can begin to implement immediately.

About the Authors

About Cheli Cerra

For more than 18 years, she has helped thousands of children achieve school and life success. As a school principal and a mother of two, Cheli knows firsthand the issues that teachers, parents and children face. She was the founding principal of one of the first K-8 schools in Miami-Dade County, Florida, Everglades Elementary. The school of 1,500 students received an A+ rating for two consecutive years under Cheli's leadership.

Cheli is the founder of Eduville, Inc., a company that provides resources and strategies for parents and teachers to help their children achieve school and life success. Among her resources are *Smarter Kid Secrets*, a free monthly e-zine, and her website **http://www.eduville.com**, full of tips, techniques and strategies useful for anyone interested in helping a child succeed.

Recognized as "The Right Choice" by *Woman's Day* magazine, and featured on over 30 radio shows throughout the country, Cheli is committed to helping teachers and parents come together for the success of children. Her seminars, coaching programs, and presentations have provided strategies that empower her audiences to action. She will captivate you by teaching the lessons learned from her in-the-trenches experience in public education. As a wife and a working mother of two, she understands the reality of everyday life and creates strategies to meet these challenges quickly and easily. Her powerful message of immigrating to this country, learning the language, and adapting to a new culture also give Cheli a unique insight into the real-world challenges children face today.

About Dr. Ruth Jacoby

Dr. Ruth is the founding principal of the Somerset Academy charter schools, which include four charter schools with 1,250 students in pre-kindergarten through ninth grade. She has more than 30 years of experience as an administrator and educator, in traditional public, private, and charter schools. Under her leadership, Somerset Charter School became one of the first charter schools to receive SACS (Southern Association of Colleges and Schools) accreditation.

Dr. Ruth received her Ed.D. degree in Child and Youth Studies for Children from Birth through 18 Years from Nova Southeastern University, and her Master of Science in Special Needs and Bachelor of Science in Early Childhood and Elementary Education from Brooklyn College.

During the past two years, Dr. Ruth has become actively involved in educating other charter school personnel in how to develop standards-based curriculum and assessments. Her school was one of the founding partners of the Tri-County Charter School Partnership, which has implemented three South Florida Annenberg Challenge grants in student assessment and school accountability and two Florida Charter School Dissemination Grants. She serves on several governing boards for charter schools in Miami-Dade County, Florida, and is an active member of the Florida Consortium of Charter Schools.

A Very Special Thanks To:

Our husbands: Tom Cerra and Marty Jacoby for their love;
Our children: Alexandra, Frank, Sari, and Scott for their patience;
Our editors: Lisa Levine, Vicki McCowan, and Paula Wallace for their thoroughness;
Our designer: Henry Corona from Corona Creative for his creative genius;
Our typist: Evelyn Thompson for her diligence;

All of the teachers and parents who have touched our lives;
Cracker Barrel, where the idea for this book was first
discussed over a cup of coffee and sugar-free apple
pie and where it continued to evolve week
after week; and **you, our reader,**
for reading, absorbing, learning,
and sharing.

"Effective communicators always leave a piece of wisdom with their audience."

To your artful and effective communication.

Cheli and Ruth

Let us hear from you . . . send us your snapshots. Email Cheli and Ruth at:

Cheli Cerra
Cheli@School-Talk.com

Ruth Jacoby
Dr.Ruth@School-Talk.com

The *School Talk!* Series
by Cheli Cerra, M.Ed. and Ruth Jacoby, Ed.D.

Parent Talk! The Art of Effective Communication With the School and Your Child

This must-have guide for parents provides 52 "snapshots" of just about every conceivable situation than can arise between a parent, a student, and a school and provides clear, simple suggestions for positive solutions. From "My child's friend is a bad influence" to "I don't understand the results from my child's test," it covers all the typical events in a student's school experience.

ISBN 0-471-72013-5   **Paperback**   **www.josseybass.com**

Teacher Talk! The Art of Effective Communication

"An amazing compilation of what to say to parents. This book is a must have for your professional library."

—*Harry K. Wong, Ed.D., author of the bestselling* The First Days of School

An essential guidebook for all teachers that presents effective strategies for handling 52 common situations and simple ways to communicate with students, parents, and administrators. Features worksheets, checklists, sample letters, and more.

ISBN 0-471-72014-3   **Paperback**   **www.josseybass.com**

Principal Talk! The Art of Effective Communication in Successful School Leadership

Principal Talk! provides simple communication strategies and advice to keep teachers, students, parents, staff, and the community in your corner. A must-read for today's educational leader to be successful in today's reform climate.

—*Jack Canfield, co-author,* Chicken Soup for the Teacher's Soul

This user-friendly, quick reference presents 52 "snapshots" of communication issues faced by busy principals and assistant principals in working with staff, parents, teachers, and the community.

ISBN 0-7879-7911-2   **Paperback**   **www.josseybass.com**

School Board Talk! The Art of Effective Communication

For both the aspiring and the veteran school board members, this book offers tips, worksheets, and practical advice to help board members develop and improve communication skills, survive in political office, and make a difference in education. In its user-friendly, easy-to-browse pages you'll find 50 "snapshots" and solution strategies on topics such as: casting the lone "no" vote and surviving, keeping your family in your fan club, building a school board team, handling constituent calls, and conquering the e-mail and memo mountain.

ISBN 0-7879-7912-0   **Paperback**   **www.josseybass.com**